# JAVA AND SQL

## A Programmer's Guide

---

**Malcolm Taylor**

# Web Site

A web site with further information about this book, including reviews and feedback, can be found at www.javasql.co.uk.

ISBN 978-0-9556763-0-7

*To Diana*

# About the Author

Malcolm Taylor graduated from the University of Cambridge in 1980 with a degree in Mathematics, and earned a Diploma in Computer Science the following year. In 1985 he received a Ph.D. from the University of Aberdeen for his thesis entitled *Data Integration and Query Decomposition in Distributed Databases*. He subsequently held academic positions at the University of Keele and the University of Houston, and was a member of the technical staff at the MCC research lab in Austin, Texas. He has been developing object-oriented software for 15 years, in which time he has worked for leading organisations in both the U.S. and U.K. in application domains including telecommunications, oil and gas, healthcare and taxation. He lives in Staffordshire, U.K., with his wife, Diana.

# CONTENTS

# 9 Java database connectivity    183

# 10  Accessing collections and large objects from Java   207

# Index of concepts    229

# Chapter 1

# INTRODUCTION

---

Companies, government departments and individuals are all needing to manage vast amounts of information, of increasingly diverse forms. As the demand for information increases, so inevitably does the complexity of the computer systems which are required to manage that information. To deal with this complexity, we are constantly seeking to improve the tools which are used to build the computer systems of today.

A modern software application often contains many different components, each using different tools and technologies. But most applications share two common requirements:
- a *database management system*, to securely store the data and allow shared access by many concurrent users
- a *programming language*, in which to display information to the user and to build the logic for processing user requests

In processing user requests, the application will typically need to retrieve existing information from the database and write new information to the database. Thus, an important requirement of the programming language is to issue requests to the database management system to store or retrieve specific information. So the two tools must not only be good for carrying out their own responsibilities, they must also be able to interoperate effectively with one another.

Both programming languages and database management systems come in many different forms, each designed to address a different set of problems. At the time of writing, though, there is a broad consensus that two specific approaches are suitable for the widest range of applications:

- Java has become the most popular programming language
- The most popular database management systems are those based on the relational data model, of which all the leading examples use SQL as the language for data access

Java and SQL have therefore become two of the most important languages for software professionals to know and understand. Yet the two are intrinsically very different. Java is an *object-oriented* language, in which a program is built as a collaboration of objects of different types. The structure of an object can be of almost arbitrary complexity: it can be as simple as a number or a string, or it may contain references to numerous other objects or even to collections of other objects. SQL, on the other hand, is based on the *relational data model*, which is the most restrictive of all the leading data models in terms of the data structures it allows. The *first normal form* constraint essentially restricts the relational model to representing data in the form of simple tables, in which each row describes an entity and each column represents a property of that entity. The values in each column must be simple values such as numbers or strings: complex values such as collections or structured objects are not allowed. To appreciate why two seemingly contradictory models of data have become popular, the one in the database world and the other in the programming language world, let us first take a look at the way languages have evolved over the past several decades.

## 1.1 Evolution of programming languages

The earliest computers had to be programmed using machine code. The instructions were sequences of binary bits, each instruction specifying manipulation of particular memory locations. An instruction could move data from one location to another, or perform some simple processing on data. But processing options were limited, because all data were essentially of the same kind – a sequence of binary bits.

The first advance was in the development of assembly languages. These still required the programmer to directly manipulate specific memory locations but, instead of writing in binary, they could at least express the instructions in a language made up of words.

Machine code and assembler are known as *low-level languages*, because they require the programmer to express instructions in terms of the computer's architecture. A major advance in programming languages came with the idea of *high-level languages*, which allowed the programmer to work at a more abstract level. Instead of thinking in the machine's terms, the programmer could express operations on variables appropriate to the problem being solved. A range of different data types could be built in to the language, and operations provided which were appropriate to the specific data type being used. This provided the programmer with far more powerful tools for expressing more complex programs. The downside, of course, was that the program would need to be translated into machine code before it could be executed on the computer. But this was accomplished by the provision of automatic programming language compilers. The compiler might not generate such efficient machine code as an expert programmer could, but the improvement in programmer productivity would more than compensate for slower execution time in most cases. Where a program needed to run as fast as possible, it remained necessary to write in low-level languages – but those cases became increasingly rare, especially as computer hardware became faster and cheaper and the demands of applications became higher.

The first high-level languages emerged in the late 1950s. For the scientific community, Fortran (Formula Translation) was developed as a tool for building number-crunching applications. Problems of numerical analysis in physics and engineering were especially suited to Fortran, and indeed it is still used in those fields today. Meanwhile, Cobol (Common Business-oriented language) was being developed as a high-level language for business data processing applications. Cobol defined record structures for data representation, and a verbose syntax for expressing operations. Cobol was very widely used for developing business applications for many years, and there are plenty of legacy applications which are still in use today in large organisations across the world.

Viewed from today's perspective, both Fortran and Cobol look like tools of computing's Stone Age. But only a few years afterwards, a much more sophisticated language emerged. Algol 60 was the first real general-purpose high-level language, designed to meet the requirements of both scientific and business applications. It introduced many of the concepts of structured programming which are still important today, such as block structure and scope rules for identifiers; more general constructs for branching and iteration; dynamic sizing of arrays; and recursive procedures. Moreover, the language was very elegantly defined using the Backus-Naur form, named after two of its creators. Ironically, very few large applications were ever built using Algol 60. It is one of the paradoxes of computing that the best technological solution is rarely the one which achieves greatest success in the marketplace. More commonly, the best ideas are carried on into future products, some of which do achieve commercial success. So it is with Algol 60, whose influence can be clearly seen in later languages such as Pascal and C, and indeed in Java.

Another unusual accomplishment of Algol 60 was to be a successful language developed by a committee. Languages designed by committees tend to suffer from bloat and, when a language is too large, it becomes cumbersome and difficult to learn. There are too many ways of doing things, and too many wrong ways of doing them. This was the problem with the next product of the Algol committee, the language known as Algol 68. Two members of the committee, Niklaus Wirth and Tony Hoare, were quick to recognise the danger of such an approach and broke away to design the much simpler Algol W. Wirth later went on to develop Pascal, which for many years was the most popular language for teaching programming concepts in universities around the world.

By the 1970s, the virtues of structured programming were widely accepted, though the investment in Fortran and Cobol was such that those two languages remained dominant commercially for some years to come. When the commercial world was ready to move to the next generation of languages in a big way, it is perhaps a little ironic that the next successful language was C. C inherited a number of structured programming features from Algol and Pascal, but it also has some low-level features. Data typing is not so strictly enforced in C, and the programmer can access memory via pointers. This can be very useful in systems programming, but can lead to a variety of run-time errors, especially in the hands of inexperienced programmers.

Another important development in the 1970s was the idea of *object-oriented programming*. Whereas a procedural language divides a program into a set of data structures and a set of procedures which act on those data structures, an object-oriented language divides a program into a set of classes such that each class *encapsulates* both a data structure and a set of algorithms (called *methods*) which act specifically on that data structure. Because the class contains both the data and the methods, there is greater scope for code reuse. A class which was developed for one application may turn out to be valuable for a completely different type of application. Moreover, a new class can be created as an extension of an existing class, in which case it automatically *inherits* all the data and methods of the original class. But perhaps the most important contribution of object-oriented programming is the notion of *polymorphism*, which allows programs to be written in terms of an abstract interface. Programs can thus be written in such a way that they are not tied to an explicit class, but rather can make use of any class which implements the interface.

One of the first object-oriented languages was Smalltalk, developed by a group including Alan Kay and Adele Goldberg at Xerox Palo Alto Research Centre. Smalltalk provides a very pure implementation of object-oriented concepts, in which everything is an object and all objects are treated in the same way. Even the browser tools, used for developing Smalltalk code, are objects like any other. The semantics of a Smalltalk program is defined in terms of a virtual machine, which allows a program developed on one platform to be deployed on another without any rewriting or recompilation of the code. Memory management is simplified by the use of garbage collectors, which periodically identify unused objects and reclaim their space. Smalltalk briefly became very popular during the 1990s, and some highly successful applications were built: some of which are still in use today. Yet by 1997, it was very much on the wane, having been overtaken by the sudden popularity of Java.

Despite its many strengths, Smalltalk also had some significant disadvantages. Firstly, there was its use of dynamic binding. Variables in Smalltalk are not declared as being instances of a specific class, so type checking needs to be done at runtime. This slows down the execution of the program and can lead to undesirable runtime exceptions. Secondly, the insistence on everything being an object creates additional execution overheads and sometimes leads to some rather unwieldy syntax. Thirdly, the difficulty of interfacing Smalltalk to C tended to make it hard to connect to external systems. And fourthly, the much-vaunted code portability did not always work quite as smoothly as expected, because the user interface might look different on certain platforms.

Bjarne Stroustrup took a rather different approach with his design of C++. His starting point was C, and he extended that language to allow the definition of classes. C++ is a huge language, and allows for a wide variety of programming styles. At one extreme, a programmer can develop an object-oriented program with classes, inheritance, polymorphism and dynamic binding. At the other extreme, a C program can be written. In practice, most C++ programmers write code which falls somewhere in between those two extremes. Classes are used to partition the code into more manageable units, but dynamic binding is not used except for virtual classes and methods. C++ is strongly typed, making it much more type safe than either Smalltalk or C. The distinction between objects and primitive values means that simple computations can be performed more efficiently. And of course, the interface to C is straightforward.

C++ continues to have its advocates, and remains widely used. But its complexity often leads to the development of code which is poorly structured and hard to maintain. Moreover, although it incorporates some object-oriented features, it is not an object-oriented language in the true sense. Java was designed to incorporate the best aspects of both C++ and Smalltalk, while eradicating their weakest features. From C++ it took a great deal of syntax, as well as strong typing and the concept of primitive types which are distinct from objects. But Java is a much smaller language, designed to fully support object-oriented development. From Smalltalk it borrows the idea of the virtual machine, garbage collection and cross-platform portability. Although syntactically it is closer to C++, Java is in many ways much closer to Smalltalk. The most obvious difference is Java's use of strong typing, which allows for more compile-time checking as well as the explicit declaration of interfaces.

Besides the strength of its design, the timing of its introduction was also in Java's favour. Emerging at a time when the internet boom was getting underway, the language was enhanced by the addition of features for supporting internet-based applications, which greatly added to its popularity.

## 1.2 Evolution of database systems

Just as programming languages have evolved through several generations, adding greater degrees of abstraction over time, so a similar development can be seen in database management systems. The earliest computer programs each ran with their own dedicated data sets but, with the advent of Cobol and business applications, it soon became necessary to find ways to support shared access to persistent data. In the 1960s, systems such as IMS and IDMS were developed to allow record-at-a-time navigation of data by (predominantly) Cobol programs. Related records were linked together in various ways, and indexed to support particular access paths to the data. Details of the physical organisation of the data were made available to application programmers, who could use this information to determine efficient ways of navigating to the information they required. These early database systems were not based on any formal data model: it was only later that the hierarchical data model and network data model were defined as a piece of reverse engineering.

A problem with the early database systems was that there was no clean separation between the database and the application program. Application programs were heavily dependent on the physical organisation of the data, in order to navigate through the records. Consequently, any reorganisation of the data was liable to invalidate application programs. It became apparent that the next generation of database systems would need to support *data independence*. Applications would need to specify the data they required in a high-level way, and the system would be responsible for choosing the access paths to those data. If the physical organisation of the data changed, the system would automatically find different strategies for accessing the same data. The question was, how could this goal be accomplished ?

The great breakthrough was accomplished by Edgar Codd of IBM, who designed the relational model of data. Codd used the mathematical concept of a relation, as used in set theory, to define a data structure that would hold a set of records. He then defined a language based on predicate calculus, which he called the *relational calculus*, to express queries against those structures. Further, he specified a set of operations, which he called the *relational algebra*, which were sufficient to implement those queries. In this model, the application programmer was no longer responsible for navigating between individual records. Instead, the relational calculus allowed set-at-a-time access to the data. The programmer would specify the data of interest in a declarative way, and the system would find a way to access those data.

Still, a number of doubts remained to be addressed. The model looked fine in theory, but it had not been tested in practice. Any implementation of the model would need to be very sophisticated if it was to process requests as efficiently as could the existing database systems. The adequacy of the relation as a data structure was also questioned. Codd had defined a *first normal form* for relations, which essentially meant that each relation could be represented as a table of simple values. Any complex record types would therefore need to be broken down into multiple tables. Further study of the model gave rise to second and third normal forms, which required an even larger number of tables to be used. So a query which requested data concerning only one or two entities might nevertheless access several different tables. Data from these tables would need to be combined using the *join* operation of Codd's relational algebra. It was clear that efficient implementations of the join were imperative, if the relational model was to succeed.

During the 1970s, a number of prototype relational database systems were developed in research laboratories around the world. The most significant of these was System R, which was developed at the IBM Laboratories. The System R team developed innovative solutions in a number of areas, including query optimisation and transaction management, which greatly influenced the subsequent commercial development of systems like DB2 and Oracle. It demonstrated that relational database systems were a practical proposition, and encouraged database vendors to make the necessary investment in the technology. But of all the important contributions made by System R, probably the most significant of all was the development of a new kind of query language which they called SEQUEL (Structured English QUEry Language). SEQUEL was defined in a rather ad hoc fashion, and was quite different from both the relational algebra and relational calculus. But the System R team had introduced the language to users and found that it was not only powerful but, crucially, was relatively easy to use. When relational products arrived on the market, most of them adopted SEQUEL as the query language. By this time the name had been shortened to SQL, but the language was essentially the same and the original pronunciation was retained. SQL became the de facto standard and, eventually, even those vendors who had promoted their own languages (notably Ingres) were forced to adopt SQL as their query language.

During the 1980s, relational database systems evolved from an experimental technology to become the dominant solution for managing persistent data. But this position of dominance was soon questioned as object-oriented programming became popular and businesses became interested in managing information with a more complex structure. An *impedance mismatch* was identified between the highly expressive object-oriented programming languages and the simple but restricted data structures supported by relational database systems. Solutions to the mismatch were sought from two distinct directions. One approach was to design an entirely new type of database system which directly implemented the object-oriented programming model. The other was to extend the relational model to support a wider range of data types and some object-like features. Each approach had its advantages. The principal attraction of object-oriented database systems was that it would completely eliminate the impedance mismatch between programming language and database language. That should make application development faster and the applications themselves more efficient. On the other hand, relational databases were a proven technology and companies had invested heavily in them. If they could be adapted to meet the new requirements, relational products were likely to retain strong support.

Accordingly, the main relational database vendors set about enhancing their products with object-oriented features. Meanwhile, a number of start-up companies brought out object-oriented database systems. These new products supported two ways of accessing data. There was a query language to provide SQL-like access; and navigational mechanisms to allow access from one object to a another using inter-object references. The idea was that application programs could be constructed by embedding queries into an object-oriented programming language. The most important of the new query languages was OQL, which was developed for the $O_2$ database system. It used a SQL-like syntax, but was able to query object structures rather than relations. Within the Smalltalk community, the GemStone database system became popular. With GemStone, applications could be built using Smalltalk on the database server as well as for the client application. Smalltalk thus became a powerful database programming language, and the application could be split so that some parts ran on the client and some on the server. Moreover, there was a garbage collector

10

which could be run on the database to remove obsolete objects. Many large applications were developed using object-oriented databases in the 1990s, and some of them were very successful. However, the technology was not as straightforward to use as many people had envisaged. There were plenty of pitfalls, which could only be avoided if the development team had a detailed understanding of the workings of the database system. Frequently, an application would run efficiently while the size of the database remained small, but would run into serious problems as the database grew. And the database administration tools were very limited in comparison with those found in earlier database products, which made it harder to identify and fix the cause of a problem. After some initial bad experiences, many users decided to abandon their experiment with object-oriented databases and concentrate on making their applications work with their existing relational database systems.

By the end of the 1990s, Java had become the dominant object-oriented programming language. With Java came a set of standardised interfaces known as Java Database Connectivity (JDBC), which provided a powerful and fairly straightforward way of accessing relational databases from a Java application. Java and SQL became a powerful combination of languages, adopted by many organisations for applications of all sizes. At the time of writing, there is no sign of either language being displaced from its position of pre-eminence.

**1.3 Application architectures**

Java applications can be built in either two or three tiers. A typical two-tier architecture, based on the Java Standard Edition (J2SE), consists of a thick client on one machine connecting to a database tier on a server machine. A typical three-tier architecture, based on the Java Enterprise Edition (J2EE) consists of a thin client connecting to a thick middle tier on a dedicted Java server, which in turn connects to an enterprise information systems tier on a database server.

In a two-tier architecture, all of the Java code resides on the client. The application designers will typically divide the application into layers of classes as follows:
- A GUI layer consisting of classes for handling the user interface

- A business logic layer consisting of classes for implementing the business logic of the application
- A persistence layer consisting of classes for interfacing between the database and the business logic layer

It is possible for these layers to be further sub-divided, particularly in larger applications.

The two tier approach is suitable for building small or medium-sized applications, which are only expected to support a small number of concurrent users. For larger applications, however, and those which are required to handle hundreds or even thousands of concurrent users, the three-tier architecture is preferred. This architecture is highly scalable because the middle tier can be physically distributed over several machines if required. A three-tiered J2EE application consists of *containers* and *components*. The containers are re-usable infrastructure which implements some of the hardest aspects of a large application:

- Multi-threading
- Managing pools of database connections
- Database transaction management
- Security

The application developers need to implement components, each of which is added to a container.

The task of building a three-tier application is quite different from that of building a two-tier application, because some of the infrastructure is provided by the containers. Nevertheless, J2EE is based on exactly the same language as J2SE – it just provides some additional classes. So whichever architecture you are using, you need to understand the same fundamentals of the Java language. If you are working on the interface between Java and the database, you also need to understand SQL, and how it interacts with Java.

## 1.4 Scope of this book

This book sets out to give the reader an understanding of both Java and SQL, and an appreciation of the differences between them. It also investigates techniques for bridging the apparent incompatibilities between the two languages and building successful applications. No previous knowledge of either language is required, though the reader is assumed to have some experience of computer programming and at least a cursory understanding of database concepts. We shall introduce Java in Chapters 2 through 4, beginning with the most basic concepts but covering all the features needed to build an application which accesses a database. It is not my intention to describe the entire language: in particular, there will be hardly any mention of the user interface. Since the book is about Java and SQL, we are interested in how Java interacts with the database, rather than how it interacts with the user. Before embarking on the coverage of SQL, we provide an overview of database fundamentals in Chapter 5. Chapters 6 through 8 describe SQL, starting with the simplest queries and going on to cover complex queries and stored procedures. In Chapter 8 we shall also examine extensions which have been made to the relational model to make it more object-oriented and better able to represent complex data structures. Chapter 9 describes Java Database Connectivity (JDBC) – the interface which enables a Java program to connect to a relational database, pass SQL statements to the database system, and receive the results. Finally, Chapter 10 looks at more advanced features of JDBC, which are needed for handling the complex data structures which we introduced in Chapter 8.

In covering database issues, my aim is to present solutions which are applicable to all the leading relational database systems. At the same time, I do not want to take a 'lowest common denominator' approach. In order to harness the full power of a product, it is frequently necessary to make use of features which are specific to that product. Where it has been necessary to illustrate a particular database system, I have chosen to use Oracle. Nevertheless, the solutions which I present for Oracle databases can generally be adapted for use with other relational databases.

# Chapter 2

# JAVA FUNDAMENTALS

---

## 2.1 Getting Started

Java is an object-oriented programming language, whose syntax is based on that of C. Consequently, it is quite straightforward for anyone who knows C to get started with programming in Java. Indeed, one of the nice features of Java is that it is not as complicated as some other languages, having relatively few constructs from which to build a program. Another feature is that a program is divided into units, and these units can be re-used across many different programs.

The smallest unit within a program is a *class*. We shall describe classes in more detail in subsequent chapters but, for now, we can consider a class to consist of a data structure and a set of operations on that structure. In this chapter, we shall look at developing programs within a single class. Later on, we shall look at how to sub-divide a program into multiple classes.

Because a class includes both the data and the operations on those data, classes are designed to be fairly self-contained. Nevertheless, it is frequently necessary for one class to make use of another. Java places restrictions on the way a class can be accessed from other classes, which is important for ensuring the reliability of large programs. If a class could be accessed in any way from any other class, it would be very hard to guarantee the reliability of the program. On the other hand, some closely related classes may need a greater degree of access than that granted to general classes. So related classes are grouped into *packages*. Access to different aspects of a class may be granted to classes in the same package, without allowing that same access to classes in different packages.

Before starting to develop any software in Java, it is necessary to obtain and install the Java development kit (JDK). The JDK includes the Java compiler and a complete runtime environment, which includes the virtual machine. The use of these tools will be described in the course of this chapter.

When developing a program, we create a separate file for the source code of each class. The name of the file must be the name of the class, with the extension .java. Thus, a class named Fred should be created in a file called Fred.java. Just as classes correspond to files, so packages correspond to directories. If the class Fred belongs to the package named myclasses, then the file Fred.java should be placed in the directory myclasses. This directory must itself reside within a directory which appears in the CLASSPATH environment variable. Users of Unix or Windows operating systems should be familiar with setting the PATH environment variable, and CLASSPATH is set in a similar fashion. On Windows,

set CLASSPATH=C:\projects\java\myclasses

Or, on Unix (using the C shell),

setenv CLASSPATH /home/projects/java/myclasses

Note that, by convention, the names of classes begin with upper-case letters, while the names of packages begin with lower-case letters. If the name of a class is made up of two or more words, the first letter of each word is written in upper-case while all other letters are lower-case. This convention is not enforced, but it is so widely followed that anybody familiar with Java will find your program confusing if you do not follow it.

One of the advantages provided by packages is that they help to maintain the uniqueness of class names, even in a large system incorporating classes written by many different programmers. This is because the full name of a class is actually packagename.classname. When we are writing a class, we can use the short-hand class name to refer to classes within the same package, but the full class name is required when referring to a class in a different package. In this way, we only need to ensure that class names are unique within a package: the same name can be used for two classes in different packages without ambiguity. Nevertheless, for clarity's sake, it is best to try to avoid creating two classes with the same name as far as possible.

Another unit of code in Java is what is known as an *archive*. An archive is a compressed file, with extension .jar or .zip, which contains Java classes. If your program needs to access classes which are in an archive, you can add the archive directly into the classpath. Thus, the classpath in general consists of a list of elements, each of which can be either an archive or a directory. These elements are separated by colons (in Unix) or semi-colons (on Windows platforms). Thus,

On Windows,
set CLASSPATH=
C:\projects\java\myclasses;C:\projects\java\myarchive.jar

or on Unix,
setenv CLASSPATH /home/projects/java/myclasses:
/home/projects/java/myarchive.jar

Having installed Java on your computer, the next step is to set the classpath and create the directory structure for your Java code. Once you have done that, you are ready to begin writing a first Java program.

## 2.2 A first program

Our first program will be a very simple one, which just prints out a fixed message each time it is run. It is not a very useful program, but it illustrates some of the essential features common to all Java programs. We begin by defining a package for the program, which we shall call myfirstpackage. We then need to define a class, which we shall call MyFirstClass. Thus, within the directory specified in the classpath, we create a sub-directory called myfirstpackage. We then create a text file called MyFirstClass.java within that sub-directory. The text file is going to contain the Java source code for our class.

The first line of a Java class always defines the package in which the class resides. In this case, package myfirstpackage;

As in many other programming languages, each statement in Java is followed by a semi-colon. We next declare the name of the class, which in this case is MyFirstClass. The definition of the class then follows within curly braces:

```
public class MyFirstClass
{
    // the code for the class goes here
}
```

The keyword public is used to declare that this class can be accessed from other classes if required. As we shall see later, declaring a class to be public does not necessarily mean that other classes have access to all of the internal structure of this class. We can, and generally will, place specific restrictions within the body of the class definition. But it is quite usual for a class to be declared public. The one line between the braces is a comment: it begins with the character sequence '//'.Comments can be placed anywhere within a program, to ease understanding. In this case, the comment is a reminder that we are going to have to write some actual Java code in order to have a program which we can run ! Sometimes we may need to write a comment which runs over more than one line. For those situations, an alternative syntax is provided, as follows:

```
/* This is a long comment,
which runs over more than
one line. */
```

Of course, we could have written the same comment by placing the '//' sequence at the start of each of the lines, but the alternative syntax can be a little easier to use for long comments.

Within the body of the class, we can write various *methods*. A method is the object-oriented equivalent of a function or procedure, the difference being that it is associated with a specific class. Methods in general can be given any name that is a valid Java identifier, but by convention the name should start with a lower-case letter. As with class names, when the name of the method consists of two or more words, the first letter of the second and any subsequent words should be upper-case (this style is called *camel case*). In order to run the program, we require one special method which will be executed when we run the class. That special method is always defined as follows:

```
public static void main (String[] args)
{
    // define the method body here
}
```

Note that the method must always be declared as 'public static void' if we want it to execute when we run the class. In the next chapter, when we look at creating classes with more than one method, we shall explain exactly what that declaration means, and we shall see that other methods do not need to be declared in that same way. For now, however, let us just accept that this is how we declare the main() method.

In the body of the method, in this first program we are just going to print out a simple message to the screen. Java provides a class called java.lang.System for this pupose. The package java.lang contains the most fundamental Java classes, which are used by virtually all programs. Because these classes are so frequently used, they can be referred to in any class without using the package name prefix. Thus, we can refer to the class java.lang.System as simply System. That class has a public field called out, which is the standard output stream. As we shall see later, it is unusual for a class to have public fields, but in this case it allows us to refer to the standard output stream from any class by writing System.out. We then need to invoke the println method, to tell the standard output stream that we want to print a line of text. The content of that line is included as a parameter to the println method, and is enclosed within parentheses. In Java, a literal string is enclosed within double quotes. Thus, we can write the following:

```
System.out.println ("This is my first Java program – it works !");
```

Thus, the full code for this class is as follows:

```
package myfirstpackage;

public class MyFirstClass
{
    public static void main (String[] args)
```

```
    {
        System.out.println ("This is my first Java program – it works !");
    }
}
```

Having written the program, the next task is to compile and run it, a process which we shall describe next.


## 2.3 Compiling and Running a Java program

To compile a Java class it is necessary to run the compiler, javac:

javac MyFirstClass.java

The compiler will look for a file called MyFirstClass.java in the current directory. Assuming it finds the file, it will try to compile it. If the file contains a valid Java class, it will produce a file called MyFirstClass.class in the same directory.

The compiler generates byte codes which can be run on any platform which supports the Java runtime environment. This is made possible by an abstraction called the *Java Virtual Machine*. The idea of a virtual machine was used in the implementation of Smalltalk, where a great deal of work was done to create efficient implementations. The idea is that each platform provides its own implementation of the virtual machine, which manages the translation of byte codes into the local machine code. Sun has published a standard for the Java Virtual Machine (JVM) which ensures that programs can be run on any machine which has a conformant JVM.

Once a class has been compiled, it can be run as follows:

java myfirstpackage.MyFirstClass

The virtual machine will first look for a file called MyFirstClass.class in the directory myfirstpackage (relative to the classpath). It will then execute the main() method of that class, as described above. Most JVMs will use a technique called Just-in-time compilation, by which byte codes are translated into machine code just before they are to be executed. A cache of translated code can be maintained to avoid the cost of repeatedly translating the same code.

## 2.4 Declaring and using variables

The first program simply printed out a fixed message. Usually, we need to perform some more complex processing which involves the use of variables. In Java, some variables take values which are objects, while others take values which are primitive types. In later chapters we shall look at variables which represent objects, but the main focus of this chapter will be on primitive types.

Primitive types are similar to the basic data types supported by C. They are quite limited in their expressive power, but are more efficient than objects for performing simple computations. The types supported by Java include the following:

- boolean (which allows values true and false)
- char (which allows any single character such as a letter, digit or punctuation symbol)
- int (which represents a 32-bit signed integer)
- long (which represents a 64-bit signed integer)
- short (which represents a 16-bit signed integer)
- byte (which represents an 8-bit signed integer)
- float (which represents a single-precision floating point number)
- double (which represents a double-precision floating point number)

As we shall see later, there are situations where it is necessary to supply an object rather than a primitive value. Consequently, Java provides wrapper classes in the java.lang package for each of the above types. These wrapper classes (Boolean, Character, Integer, Long, Short, Byte, Float and Double) exist solely as a means of creating objects which hold references to the primitive values, and cannot themselves be used directly in calculations.

Before using a variable in a Java program, it is necessary to declare it. The declaration specifies both the name and the type. The name can be any valid Java identifier that is not a reserved word. An identifier is made up of letters, digits, dollar signs and underscore characters, with the first character not allowed to be a digit. Reserved words are those which have a special meaning in the Java language: for example, class, package, if, for. Some examples of valid variable declarations are:

int aNumber;
char ch3;
double radius;
boolean done;

Note that, by convention, the names of variables start with a lower-case letter. It is usual to use only letters for the names of most variables, with digits and other characters being used sparingly if at all. As with classes, if a name is made up of two or more words, camel case is used. Although the use of these conventions is not enforced, it is good practice to follow them because it aids the readability of programs and enables others to easily distinguish the variables from the classes.

Assignment of a value to a variable is done using the '=' operator:

aNumber = 10;

When we assign a literal value to a variable, the usual number formats are supported for numeric types; character literals are enclosed in single quotes. The following are all legal assignments:

aNumber = -23;
ch3 = 'q';
radius = 19.57;
done = true;

Quite frequently, we need to add 1 to the value of an integer variable. This could be done by writing:

anInteger = anInteger + 1;

However, a convenient and more efficient shorthand is:

++anInteger;

This notation can also be used within a more complex statement. In that case, it means that the value of anInteger should be incremented before executing the statement. To specify that the value should be incremented after executing the statement, we should write

anInteger++;

Similarly, the operator '--' is used to decrement the value of an integer variable. More generally, for changing the value of a variable by a constant amount, we can use the += or -= operators:

anInteger += 2;

When assigning to a numeric variable, it is legal to assign a value from a more restricted type to a variable of a more general type (the system can convert the value to the more general type). Thus, we can assign a short value to a long variable, or an int to a double. But the reverse assignments would not be valid: if we try to assign long value to a short variable, for example, the conversion cannot in general be done. Note also that literal numbers are by default interpreted as being of type int or double, depending on whether a decimal point is present. To specify other numeric types, it is necessary to append a letter at the end of the number, or to make an explicit cast. Thus,

12L or (long)12 is a long value,
(short)12 is a short value,
(byte)12 is a byte value,
24.1f or (float)24.1 is a float value

The usual arithmetic operators are available for use with the numeric types (+, -, *, /). For integers, there is also the % operator which produces the remainder when one integer is divided by another. An arithmetic expression involving integer operands produces a result of type int, unless at least one of the operands is of type long, in which case the result is also a long. An explicit cast can be used to convert the value to a different integer type, for example:

```
byte byte1 = (byte)1;
byte byte2 = (byte)2;
byte byte3 = (byte)(byte1 + byte2);
```

Note that this kind of casting introduces a risk of some unexpected results because we are simply taking the least significant 8 bits. If the value of byte3 is greater than 127 or less than –128, some significant bits are being lost and the computation will not be doing an addition of integers. To see this, consider the weighting assigned to each of the eight bits in a byte value:

| -128 | 64 | 32 | 16 | 8 | 4 | 2 | 1 |
|------|----|----|----|---|---|---|---|

The largest positive integer that can be represented as a byte is 127 = 01111111. The negative integer of largest magnitude is –128 = 10000000. Adding 1 to 127, for example, will produce –128 when the result is cast to a byte.

Additional functions are provided by the class java.lang.Math, for example, Math.sqrt(aNumber) returns the square root of the number provided as parameter.

We are now ready to look at a second program. This program will compute the length of the hypotenuse of a right-angled triangle, given the length of the other two sides. We shall assume that the lengths of the two given sides are integer values, but the hypotenuse will nevertheless need to be floating point. The program will use a straightforward computation based on Pythagoras' Theorem:

$$C^2 = A^2 + B^2$$

The code for the class is shown below:

```
package myfirstpackage;

public class Hypotenuse
{
    public static void main (String[] args)
    {
        int side1 = 5;
        int side2 = 12;
        double hypotenuse = Math.sqrt(side1*side1 + side2*side2);
        System.out.println ("The hypotenuse is: " +hypotenuse);
    }
}
```

Note that Math.sqrt expects a double as parameter and returns a double as result. We are able to provide an int as parameter, because the system is able to convert an int to a double. Unlike the first program, this one is performing some computation. But its value is still limited, of course, because it always computes the same value. We could change the values assigned to the variables side1 and side2, but that would make it a different program and it would need to be recompiled. In practice, we would want the program to accept values for side1 and side2 as inputs at runtime: but that requires some additional features of Java which we shall cover later.

You will have noticed that the main() method, in each of the programs we have listed, takes a parameter whose type is String[]. This notation is used to denote an array of strings, as we shall see later. An array is an ordered collection of elements which are all of the same type. In general, we can have an array of any element type, and any length. For example, we could declare a variable intArray to be an array of integers as follows:

int[] intArray;

Note that the declaration does not specify the length of the array. That is specified only when the array is created. We shall describe the use of arrays in more detail later.

Notice also the use of the '+' operator in specifying what is to be printed. In this case, because we have put a string on the left-hand side of the '+', the operation represents string concatenation. We are going to print a literal string followed by the value of the variable hypotenuse. This approach is very frequently used in Java programs. The literal string is an instance of the class java.lang.String, which supports a variety of operations on strings. Before proceeding further, let us look into that class in a little more detail.

## 2.5 The String class

The class java.lang.String represents immutable strings of characters. By immutable, we mean that the value is assigned once and cannot be changed. If we want to add or remove characters, it is necessary to create a new string. A separate class, java.lang.StringBuffer, is provided to support operations which change the value of an object containing a string value.

24

There are two distinct ways to assign a value to a variable of type String. One way is to assign a literal string to the variable, as in the following example:

String myString = "A literal string";

Another way is to explicitly create a new string using a *constructor*. Constructors, as we shall see in the next chapter, are the usual way of creating objects: the String class is unusual in providing the alternative option described above. A constructor creates a new object and initialises it using values passed in to it. In the case of the String class, we can pass in the literal string:

String newString = new String ("A new string");

The two ways of assigning a string value are similar, but there are subtle differences. When we use a literal string, Java will cache the value internally. If we use the same literal string later, it will use the same object. When we use the constructor, on the other hand, we are always creating a new object. This has an impact on performance, because object creation has an overhead in terms of both time and space. It can also have an impact on the behaviour of the program, as we shall illustrate by the following example:

String string1 = "A string";
String string2 = "A string";
boolean sameString = (string1 == string2);
System.out.println ("The comparison between the strings gave result: " +sameString);

The comparison operator '==' returns true if its operands are *the same object*, and false otherwise. If they are different objects which happen to have the same value, it will still return false. So the above example will behave differently from this one:

String string1 = new String("A string");
String string2 = new String("A string");
boolean sameString = (string1 == string2);

System.out.println ("The comparison between the strings gave result: "
+sameString);

Whereas the first example gave a result of true, the second example gives a
result of false. This is because we are creating different objects when we
use the constructor, even though they represent the same literal string. A
different comparison operator is provided for testing whether two strings
have equal values:

boolean equalStrings = (string1.equals(string2));

Sometimes we want to consider two strings to be equal if the characters
within them match except for the case of the letters. In that case, we can use
the method equalsIgnoreCase():

String string1 = "Stoke-on-Trent";
String string2 = "STOKE-ON-TRENT";
boolean equalButForCase = string1.equalsIgnoreCase(string2);

The variable equalButForCase will be assigned the value true.

It is often necessary to obtain the length of a string, which is done using the
length() method:

int stringLength = myString.length();

To obtain the value of a specific character within the string, we need to
specify the index of that character. In Java, the first character is at index 0,
and the last character is at index string.length() – 1. So, to obtain the first
character,

char firstChar = myString.charAt(0);

To find a substring, specify the index of the first character in the substring,
and the index of the first character beyond the end of the substring. Thus

"Programmer".substring (3, 9)

would yield the string "gramme". In general, substring(i1, i2) yields a
substring of length i2-i1. Note that the second index can be omitted: the

resulting substring then consists of all characters from the first index up to the end of the string.

## 2.6 Bitwise operations

We saw in Section 2.4 how a byte represents an integer as a string of eight bits. The other integer types (short, int and long) use a similar binary representation in which the most significant bit carries a large negative weight and all other bits carry a positive weight. Sometimes it is useful to be able to manipulate the bit pattern directly, and Java provides a number of operators for doing just that. There are three operators which combine the bit patterns of two different integers:

| & | bitwise AND, producing 1 where both operands have a 1, and 0 otherwise |
| | | bitwise OR, producing 1 where at least one operand has a 1, and 0 otherwise |
| ^ | bitwise exclusive-OR, producing 1 where exactly one operand has a 1, 0 otherwise |

Thus, for example,

7 & 11 → 3
7 | 11 → 15
7 ^ 11 → 12

Another group of operators performs shift operations on the bit pattern of a single operand:

| << | Shifts all bits to the left, adding a 0 for the least significant bit |
| >> | Shifts all bits to the right, maintaining sign (i.e., the most significant bit is unchanged) |
| >>> | Shifts all bits to the right, adding a 0 for the most significant bit |

In each case, an integer can be placed to the right of the operator to indicate how many places to shift. For example,

15 << 3 → 120
15 >> 3 → 1
-1 >> 30 → -1

-1 >>> 30 → 3

Note that −1, as an int, is represented as a bit string of 32 ones. Therefore, shifting it 30 places to the right leaves only 2 ones when we use >>>, whereas >> retains all the ones.


## 2.7 Inputting data

A program is usually designed to solve a general class of problems, rather than to perform exactly the same task each time it executes. In order to make this possible, it is necessary to be able to provide input data to the program. The program can then perform different actions, depending on the data provided.

The simplest way to provide input to a program is in the command line when the program is run. For example, suppose we want to generalise the Hypotenuse class so that it will compute the length of the hypotenuse for a general right-angled triangle, rather than only one whose other two sides are of length 5 and 12. We could then provide the lengths of the two shorter sides as arguments:

java myfirstpackage.Hypotenuse 5 12

Let us now look in outline at how we might modify the main() method of the Hypotenuse class to read these command-line arguments. The values "5" and "12" which we included in the command line become elements of the array args which is the parameter of the main() method. Individual elements of an array are accessed by their position (or index) within the array. In Java, the first element of an array is in position 0, the second in position 1, and so on. There is a length function which tells us the number of elements in the array. The command-line arguments will be assigned in general to positions 0 to args.length-1 of the array args. The value of an array element is obtained by giving the array index in brackets after the name of the array. For example,

args[0]

Command-line arguments are always of type String. In the Hypotenuse class, we need to convert them into int values before they can be used in

28

calculations. This requires some additional constructs which we shall cover in the next chapter.

A more common way of providing input to a program is through the read() method of the class java.lang.InputStream. We saw earlier that System.out provides access to the standard output stream, so it will be no surprise to see that System.in provides access to the standard input stream. The InputStream class provides a method called read() which reads input into an array of bytes:

```
byte[] buf;
System.in.read(buf);
```

Having obtained the input as an array of bytes, we next need to convert it to a string. This is done as follows:

```
String inString = new String (buf);
```

This converts the data in the byte array buf into a string held in a variable called inString. At this point, we have the input data in a string variable, just as we did when entering the data as command-line arguments. But using an input stream gives us the flexibility of receiving data at any stage of the program, not just at the beginning. It also allows us to prompt the user to enter some data, which provides a more convenient interface:

```
byte[] buf;
System.out.print ("Enter the name of the person: ");
System.in.read (buf);
String personsName = new String (buf);
```

We shall describe techniques for data input in much more detail later on. In this chapter, we shall stick to simple examples which take data from the command line, if at all.

## 2.8 Conditional statements

When a program receives inputs, we may want it to take different actions depending on the values input. Conditional statements allow us to specify different branches of the program which are to be taken when certain conditions are met. The simplest type of conditional statement is the conditional assignment, in which the value assigned to a variable depends on a specified condition. The general form of this statement is:

variable = condition ? value : value;

This means that we assign the first value to the variable when the condition is true, and the second value when the condition is false. For example, suppose we want to find the absolute value of an integer held in a variable called anInteger, and to assign the value to a variable called absVal. We could write

absVal = (anInteger >= 0) ? anInteger: - anInteger;

A more general conditional statement is the if-then-else statement, which takes the following form:

```
if (condition)
    statement;
else
    statement;
```

This allows us to define any actions for the two cases of the condition being true or false, not just assignments. For example,

```
if (anInteger >= 0)
    ++anInteger;
else
    System.out.println ("anInteger is negative");
```

Sometimes we don't want to do anything in the case where the condition is false, in which case the 'else' part can be omitted altogether.

Note that the syntax demands that the action taken under each branch of the if-then-else is a single statement. This might appear to be a restriction but is not really, because we can group any number of statements into a compound statement. A compound statement is also a kind of statement, so it can be used in either of the branches. To create a compound statement, just enclose a group of statements within braces. For example,

```
if (anInteger >= 0)
{
    ++anInteger;
    System.out.println ("anInteger is positive");
}
else
    System.out.println ("anInteger is negative");
```

Comparison operators for numeric values include ==, <, <=, >, >= and !=. The == comparison evaluates to true when the two operands are equal, and the != comparison evaluates to true when the two operands are not equal. Care should be taken when dealing with floating point numbers: because in general they are not represented exactly, any comparison for equality of two floating point numbers is liable to be invalid. Instead, it is better to test whether the difference between them is less than some very small value.

More complex conditions can be formed using the logical connectives && (logical-AND) and || (logical-OR). When a logical connective is present in a condition, the right-hand operand will not be evaluated if the result is already determined by the value of the left-hand operand. This can be useful in cases where evaluation of the right-hand operand might be invalid. For example,

```
if ((x >= 0.0) && Math.sqrt(x) < 2.5)
```

We cannot evaluate the square root of x when x is negative. Fortunately, since the left-hand operand is false when x is negative, Java will not try to evaluate the right-hand operand in that case – it is already clear that the condition is false, without determining the value of the square root.

Now suppose that we want to write a method which will test the value of a character variable and print out the name of a country whose name begins with that letter. Let us assume for simplicity that the value of the character variable is known to be an upper-case letter. We could write an if-then-else statement as follows:

```
if (firstLetter == 'A')
    System.out.println ("Australia");
else if (firstLetter == 'B')
    System.out.println ("Brazil");
```

```
else if (firstLetter == 'C')
    System.out.println ("China");
else if (firstLetter == 'D')
    System.out.println ("Denmark")
else
    System.out.println ("Program only handles letters from A to D");
```

The statement is rather long and not particularly clear. It is also quite inefficient in execution. A better way of writing it is to use what is called a switch statement. The switch statement is less general than if-then-else, but is useful in cases where there are many branches, and all depend on the value of a particular variable. The above statement could be written instead in the following way:

```
switch (firstLetter)
{
    case 'A':
        System.out.println ("Australia");
        break;
    case 'B':
        System.out.println ("Brazil");
        break;
    case 'C':
        System.out.println ("China");
        break;
    case 'D':
        System.out.println ("Denmark");
        break;
    default:
        System.out.println ("Program only handles letters from A to D");
}
```

The switch statement works by evaluating the variable and executing the first case which matches. A default case is usually added at the end to handle the possibility that none of the listed values matches the variable. Note also that we have ended each case with a 'break' statement. This has the effect of breaking out of the switch statement. If no break was present, Java would go on to execute the next listed case instead of breaking out of the switch statement.

## 2.9 Looping

It is frequently necessary to execute a block of statements repeatedly until some condition becomes false. Java provides four different ways of doing this, each of which is useful in particular circumstances.

The while statement checks the condition at the start, and will not execute the block of statements at all if the condition is initially false. The syntax is

```
while (condition)
{
    // specify the block of statements here
}
```

A danger with this kind of loop is that, if the condition is initially true, it might continue to be true forever. The program will then get stuck in an infinite loop. It is important to check that the body of the loop contains a statement that can, at least potentially, transform the condition from true to false. Let us look at an example:

```
int i = 0;
while (i < 10)
{
    System.out.println ("Executing the body of the loop");
    ++i;
}
```

In the above example, the loop will continue to be executed as long as the value of i is less than 10. So once we start executing the body of the loop at least once, we are going to keep executing it unless the value of i is changed from being less than 10 to being greater than or equal to 10. So there must be within the loop body a statement which can increase the value of i. In this example, we are incrementing the value at the end of the loop body, and this will eventually cause the loop to terminate.

The second type of loop is the do-while statement, which differs from the while statement in that it has the condition at the end of the loop. Consequently it always executes the body of the loop at least once. It is probably the least used of the four types of loop, but is useful in situations

where you know that the loop needs to be executed at least once. The
general form of the statement is:

```
do
{
    // specify the block of statements here
} while (condition);
```

As with the while loop, care should be taken to ensure that the loop will
terminate.

The third type of loop is the for-loop, which is also the one which is most
frequently used. Its capabilities are very similar to those of the while loop,
but the syntax makes it a little easier to express the logic correctly. The
general form is:

```
for (initialisation; terminationCondition; increment)
    loop-body;
```

The initialisation step is used to initialise the loop. Typically it assigns an
initial value to a variable which controls the loop, but the general form is
quite flexible. The terminationCondition determines when the loop exits:
the body of the loop will be executed as long as the condition evaluates to
true. After each iteration, following execution of the loop body and before
checking the termination condition again, the increment step is executed:
typically this increments the value of the variable which controls the loop,
though it could equally be used to decrement the value. Note that a for-loop
could be expressed as an equivalent while-loop thus:

```
initialisation;
while (terminationCondition)
{
    loop-body;
    increment;
}
```

One of the advantages of the for-loop is that it expresses the logic more
naturally in cases where the loop is to be executed a known number of
times. In such cases, we can declare a variable in the initialisation step and
use that variable to control the loop. This approach has the added advantage

of limiting the scope of the variable to the loop itself, reducing the possibility of errors in the rest of the method.

As an example of the for-loop, let us consider a program which generates a sequence of pseudo-random numbers and analyses patterns within the sequence. A feature of random numbers is that each value is likely to occur equally often when a sufficiently large sample is used. However, a value should be repeated not at regular intervals but in an unpredictable distribution. Therefore, within a small or moderate-sized sample, we can expect that some values will occur more frequently than others. The program will utilise a method in the class java.lang.Math which generates pseudo-random numbers x of type double, such that $0.0 <= x < 1.0$. We are going to generate a sequence of 100 such numbers, and multiply each by 100 in order to get numbers whose integer part is in the range 0 to 99. Theoretically, each of the numbers from 0 to 99 is equally likely to occur. We shall count how many even numbers and how many odd numbers are found.

We shall define a main() method to perform the computation. It will have a for-loop whose body is executed 100 times. At each iteration, we generate a pseudo-random number, from which we obtain an integer between 0 and 99 as described above. Within the loop, we maintain a count of the even and odd numbers found. The form of the loop is

for (int i=0; i < 100; i ++)

This declares a variable i whose scope is limited to the loop. We initialise the variable to zero, and increment its value at each iteration. The loop will exit when the value of i reaches 100, so it will be executed exactly 100 times (for values of i from 0 to 99 inclusive). The method Math.random() is used to obtain a number in the range 0.0 to 1.0. Multiplying by 100 gives us a value of type double that is non-negative and less than 100.0. The method Math.floor() is then used to obtain a double value containing only the integer part of that number. We cast that value to an integer and use the % operator to obtain the remainder when the integer is divided by 2. In this way we obtain the count of odd and even numbers. The complete code for the main() method is listed below.

```
public static void main (String[] args)
{
```

```
    int evenCount = 0;
    int oddCount = 0;
    for (int i=0; i < 100; i ++)
    {
        double d = Math.random() * 100;
        int randomInt = (int)Math.floor(d);
        if (randomInt % 2 == 0)
            ++ evenCount;
        else
            ++ oddCount;
    }
    System.out.println ("Even count: "+evenCount+", Odd count:"
        +oddCount);
}
```

The fourth type of loop is the for-each loop, which is specifically designed for iterating over arrays and collections. Before describing that loop, we need to say a little more about arrays.


## 2.10 Arrays

Very often, we need to keep track of a number of related data items of the same type. Rather than having to declare separate variables for each, it is useful to be able to declare them as an array so that we can easily define operations over the full collection of values. In Java, an array is characterised by the following properties:

- all elements of an array must be of the same type: this can be either a primitive type or a class
- declaration of an array defines the element type but not the number of elements; space is not allocated for the array until it is actually created
- when we create an array we do need to fix the size; once it is created we cannot add or remove elements
- individual elements of an array are accessed by an integer index which starts at 0 and runs to length-1, where length is the number of elements in the array

Let us now illustrate these properties through some examples. The following are valid array declarations:

```
int[] numArray;
String[] wordArray;
```

To create the array, we use the new method:

```
numArray = new int[20];
wordArray = new String[10];
```

In the above examples, numArray will be initialised to all zeroes (because all integer variables are initialised to zero) whereas wordArray is not initialised. All object-typed variables should be explicitly initialised before they are read: value-typed variables are initialised automatically, but sometimes it is necessary to add explicit re-initialisation in order to assign different values.

Suppose we want to initialise wordArray so that its ten elements all have the value of the empty string. One way of doing this would be to define a for-loop to iterate over all the valid indices of the array. Thus,

```
for (int i=0; i < 10; i++)
    wordArray[i] = "";
```

For versions of the JDK up to 1.4, this is the accepted way to iterate over an array. It works, and is reasonably clear, and in this simple example it is probably quite safe. In general, though, using indices to iterate over an array is dangerous, because there is always the risk of using an index which is out of the valid range, causing the program to fail. JDK version 5 therefore introduced a new kind of loop, specifically for iterating over arrays and other kinds of collections. This for-each loop uses the syntax shown below:

```
for (w : wordArray)
    w = "";
```

This should be read as "for each w in wordArray, set the value of w to the empty string". The syntax is clear and concise, and much safer. The most common mistake that is made when accessing arrays is to calculate the index values incorrectly. By using a syntax which avoids explicit use of the index at all, we avoid this risk.

Let us now look at a program to generate prime numbers less than some set limit. We shall use 1000 as the limit, but the program is easily modified to use a different limit. The technique that we shall employ is known as the sieve of Eratosthenes. The idea behind it is that, if a number is not prime, it must have at least one prime factor that is less than the square root of the limit. So it uses an array of boolean values to indicate which numbers are prime, and starts out by setting all of them to be prime. Then for each potential prime factor, it generates all multiples of that prime factor which are less than the limit, and deduces that none of the resulting numbers can be prime. After all potential factors have been considered, those numbers which are still set to be prime must indeed be primes. The complete code is as follows

```
public static void main (String[] args)
{
    boolean[] isPrime = new boolean[1000];
    for (boolean b: isPrime)
        b = true;
    isPrime[0] = false;
    isPrime[1] = false;
    for (int divisor = 2; divisor*divisor < 1000; divisor++)
    {
        // numbers divisible by divisor are not prime
        if (isPrime[divisor])
          for (int factor = divisor; factor*divisor < 1000; factor++)
            isPrime [factor*divisor] = false;
    }
    for (int i = 0; i < 1000; i++)
        if (isPrime[i])
            System.out.println (""+i+ " is prime");
}
```

Note that we have used a for-each loop to initialise the array to all true values. If using version 1.4 or earlier, we would instead use a for-loop. Note also that we only need to generate the product factor*divisor once, which is why the inner loop is initialised with factor=divisor – we are deliberately generating only those pairs (factor and divisor) with factor >= divisor.

Our next loop example tests a word to see whether or not it is a palindrome, i.e., a word which reads the same backwards as forwards. We shall enter the word as a command-line input, and use the charAt() method described in Section 2.5 to check the value of specific characters. We need to check that the first character is the same as the last character; that the second character is the same as the penultimate character; and so on, until either we reach the middle of the word and all relevant pairs have been found to match, or we find a pair somewhere which do not match. We need to be a little more precise about what we mean by reaching the middle of the word. If the word has an even number of characters, say 2N, then we check index i against index 2N-1-i for values of i from 0 to N-1. If the word has an odd number of characters, say 2N+1, then we check index i against index 2N-i for values of i from 0 to N-1. Note that, in the latter case, the final check involves index N-1 against index N+1, meaning that the character at index N will not be checked. That is fine, because it is the middle character and would only be compared with itself if we continued for one more step. The code for the main() method of the Palindrome class is shown below:

```
public static void main (String[] args) {
    if (args.length < 1)
        System.out.println ("Insufficient arguments specified");
    else
    {
        String w = args[0];
        boolean isP = true;
        int len = w.length();
        for (int i=0; isP && (i < len/2); i++)
            if (w.charAt(i) != w.charAt(len-1-i))
                isP = false;
        if (isP)
            System.out.println (w+" is a palindrome");
        else
            System.out.println (w+" is not a palindrome");
    }
}
```

As we saw in Section 2.7, the array args consists of the command-line arguments used to run the program. We are depending on there being an argument given, because the program is going to check whether that word is a palindrome. Nevertheless, we need to allow for the possibility that the user will forget to specify a command-line argument. Therefore we check the length of the args array at the beginning, before deciding whether the program can proceed. If an argument is found, we initialise our check to true and proceed to test each pair of characters as described above. The checking continues until either a non-matching pair is found or we reach the middle of the word. Note that the condition was i <= N-1 (or, equivalently, i < N) where the length of the string was either 2N or 2N+1. In the loop termination condition, we are using integer division which throws away any fractional part: thus, (2N+1)/2 will yield N.

## 2.11 Regular Expressions

A regular expression is a pattern which defines a collection of strings composed from a given alphabet. More precisely, it is composed from the following constructs:

- $\epsilon$, the empty string
- x, a single character from the alphabet
- XY, a concatenation of a string in X and a string in Y
- X | Y, a choice between a string in X and a string in Y
- X*, a concatenation of zero or more strings in X

Regular expressions defined in this way are important, because they define languages which can be recognised by a finite state machine. They arise in many areas of computer science and are supported by various languages, including Java. Very often some additional constructs are permitted, which do not allow any additional languages to be expressed but which do allow some expressions to be written more concisely. An example is X+, meaning a concatenation of one or more strings from X. It is clear that X+ can be equivalently expressed as XX*, but the shorter form allows us to write expressions more succinctly. To avoid the need for $\epsilon$, there are constructs which allow for an optional string: X? means zero or one occurrence of a string from X.

The class java.lang.String implements a method called matches(), which tests whether or not the string matches a given regular expression. The regular expression is a string-valued parameter of the method, and is expressed using the constructs listed above and some further extensions. In Java, we can use A-Z to denote an upper-case letter, a-z to denote a lower-case letter.

Let us look now at a program which receives a person's name as a string and validates that the name is properly formatted. For the purposes of this example, we consider only the last name of a person, and we assume that the name starts with an upper-case letter and uses lower-case subsequently. Single-letter names are not allowed, so we can consider a name to consist of an upper-case letter followed by one or more lower-case letters. This can be expressed as a regular expression thus:

[A-Z][a-z]+

Next, we would like to allow for a prefix of O', Mc or Mac. The prefix is optional, so we need to allow the possibility of the empty string as prefix. Thus,

[O'|Mc|Mac]?[A-Z][a-z]+

Finally, we allow for double-barrelled names which are formed using two expressions of the above form, with a dash between them. Thus, we can have either the above form or this one:

[O'|Mc|Mac]?[A-Z][a-z]+- [O'|Mc|Mac]?[A-Z][a-z]+

The complete main() method is shown below:

```
public static void main(String[] args) {
    if (args.length < 1)
        System.out.println ("Insufficient arguments in command line");
    else
    {
        String toCheck = args[0];
        if (toCheck.matches ("[O'|Mc|Mac]?[A-Z][a-z]+") ||
          toCheck.matches (
            "[O'|Mc|Mac]?[A-Z][a-z]+-[O'|Mc|Mac]?[A-Z][a-z]+"))
            System.out.println (toCheck+" is a valid name");
        else
            System.out.println (toCheck+" is not a valid name");
    }
}
```

# Chapter 3

# OBJECT-ORIENTED PROGRAMMING IN JAVA

In the previous chapter, we presented the structure of the simplest types of Java program, in which all of the code is created in a single file. This approach is limited to very small programs, and clearly does not scale to the development of large-scale software. In this chapter, we shall look at ways of structuring a Java program so that it can be easily maintained and extended.

Java is based on the object-oriented paradigm, which encourages a different way of structuring programs from the earlier, procedural languages. An object-oriented program involves a collection of objects which cooperate to carry out the tasks required. Each object is an instance of a *class*, which determines not only the structure of the object but the activities that it can carry out. The key to developing good object-oriented software is to identify the right set of classes, and the right interactions between objects of different classes – a process known as object-oriented design. Let us now look at the features which Java provides for supporting object-oriented development.

## 3.1 Classes

A Java program consists of a number of classes, each usually in its own file. Each class has associated with it a number of variables, which hold data required by instances of the class, and operations, which implement the tasks which instances of the class are required to carry out. In a pure object-oriented model, a class is also an object: it is an instance of a meta-class. Thus, there are variables and operations associated with the class itself, as well as those associated with instances of the class. Variables and operations associated with instances of the class are known as instance variables and instance methods, respectively. Those associated with the class itself are known as class variables and class methods. All are defined within the same file, as part of the class definition.

## 3.2 Encapsulation

One of the key concepts in object-oriented programming is the idea of encapsulation. This means that the data held by an object are hidden from instances of other classes. Objects can read or modify their own data directly, but when they access other objects they do so via well-defined high-level interfaces. This has several advantages for building large-scale, reliable applications which can be easily maintained:

- The implementation of a class can change without affecting other classes, so long as the public interface remains the same.
- Developers of other classes do not need to understand the details of a class's implementation in order to use the class, they only need to know its public interface
- Code to access the internal data will only be written once, even though it may be invoked from many other classes.

The importance of encapsulation for large-scale software development has been recognised for a long time, but it is with the advent of object-oriented programming that it has received widespread acceptance. Java provides features which support and encourage encapsulation. Although it does not enforce their use, it is good practice to use encapsulation in the development of all classes.

Let us suppose that we wish to develop a program which will display geometric shapes in different locations on the screen. We might decide to create a class called LineSegment, which is responsible for displaying a line segment. A line segment is defined by its two end points, so we might use a class called Point to represent the end points. Thus,

```
package example.geometric;

public class Point
{

  // define instance variables here
  protected double x; // x coordinate
  protected double y; // y coordinate

  // define constructors
  public Point (double xVal, double yVal)
  {
    x = xVal;
    y = yVal;
  }

  // define instance methods


  public String toString()
  {
    return ""+x+'@'+y;
  }

  double distanceTo (Point aPoint)
  {
    return Math.sqrt ((x-aPoint.x)*(x-aPoint.x) + (y-aPoint.y)*(y-aPoint.y));
  }

  public static void main (String[] args)
  {
    Point p1 = new Point (1.0, 2.0);
    Point p2 = new Point (4.0, 6.0);
    Double dist = p1.distanceTo (p2);
    System.out.println ("The distance between " + p1 + " and " + p2 + " is "
        + dist);
  }

}
```

Let us examine each part of this class definition in turn. The first line of any class definition is the package statement. In this case, the package is example.geometric, which means that the file containing the class definition will reside in the directory example/geometric (on Unix platforms) or example\geometric (on Windows platforms) relative to the classpath. Next we specify the name of the class, which (by convention) should normally begin with an upper-case letter. We are calling the class Point, which means that the source code for the class will reside in a file named Point.java. We are declaring the class to be public, meaning that it should be accessible by any other class in whatever package.

The next stage is to define the data for the class: in this case, we do not need any class variables so we only define instance variables. The instance variables hold the coordinates of the point on the screen, so they are given the primitive type double. They are declared protected, for reasons which will be explained later .

Having declared the variables, we next define one or more constructors for the class. A constructor is used to create new instances of the class, a subject on which we shall expand a little later.

After the constructors come the methods for the class. Again, this class does not require any class methods so we simply define the instance methods. The first instance method is called toString, and is used to define how an instance of the class should be displayed as a string. This is an important method which should be defined for any class where we may want to display instances as strings. A default implementation is provided if we do not explicitly define one, but the default usually does not display instances in the way we would like to see them. Note that the names of methods begin (by convention) with a lower case letter. If the name comprises more than one word, the words are concatenated without separators but each word after the first one should start with an upper case letter. We define the method to be public, meaning that it can be invoked from any class, in any package. We define its return type as String, because it will return the string representation of the object. Any method which returns a value must have a return type: a method which returns no value is declared with return type void. The body of the method consists, in this case, of just one statement. That statement begins with the reserved word return, indicating that it is where we return the result of the method. The result is formed by concatenating several strings, the first of which is the empty string. Use of the empty string in this situation allows us to use + as a concatenation operator with arguments of any type. Note that + is an overloaded operator, whose meaning is determined by the type of its left-hand operand. Because the first operand is a string, we are able to concatenate a double, a character and another double. In this case they are all primitive values, but in general we can also concatenate objects which are instances of classes. In that case, the objects would be displayed using the result of their toString() methods.

The next method is called distanceTo, and it takes an argument called aPoint which is also an instance of the Point class. The purpose of this method is to compute the distance from a point to some other specified point. In this case the return type is double, because we are returning the distance between two points. Notice also that we have not declared this method to be public. This means that the method can be invoked only from within other classes of the same package. Again the body of the method consists only of the return statement, and this time the value is computed as the square root of the square of the difference between the x-coordinates of the points plus the square of the difference between their y-coordinates. The sqrt function is a class method on the Math class, which is in the java.lang package. Because it is a class method, we invoke it by writing the name of the class followed by a dot and the name of the method. The argument is the value whose square root we want to compute..

## 3.3 Access modifiers

In defining a class, each variable or method can be assigned an access modifier, which specifies which other classes are able to access that variable or method. The supported access modifiers are:

- private, meaning that access is allowed only from within the class in which the variable or method is defined
- package, meaning that access is also allowed from any class in the same package
- protected, which means that access is allowed from any class which is either a subclass or is in the same package as the one in which the variable or method is defined
- public, which allows access from anywhere

Package access is the default which applies when no access modifier is given. To provide encapsulation, all variables should ideally be declared as private. This is the only way to be sure that the data cannot be accessed by other classes, though sometimes in practice it is necessary to relax the requirement of full encapsulation by defining protected variables. Methods can be declared using any access level modifier, but the public methods should be those which perform the general behviour which the class is required to expose. Public methods should not reveal the underlying implementation, but should be such that they will retain the same interface even if the implementation changes.

Sometimes it is useful to define variables which are local to a particular method or block. Such local variables have a scope which is limited to the block in which they are declared. When the program exits that block, they become out of scope and cannot be referred to. In the previous example of the Point class, the variables p1, p2 and dist are local to the main() method. Note that local variables (unlike instance variables and class variables) have no access modifiers because they have no meaning outside the context of the block or method in which they are declared.

### 3.4 Constructors

A class will usually include one or more constructors,which are responsible for initialising instance variables when an instance of the class is created. A constructor is like a method, but with some significant differences:
- A constructor has no return type
- A constructor has the same name as the class. Consequently, by convention, it generally begins with an upper-case letter whereas method names start with lower-case letters
- A constructor is not invoked directly, but rather as a side-effect of invoking the 'new' method. Invoking 'new' creates a new instance of the class and invokes a constructor with whatever arguments were passed to 'new'.
- A constructor can invoke other constructors of the same class, but only in the first line of the constructor.

There are some other issues of constructors relating to superclasses and inheritance – see later.

## 3.5 Field modifiers

Variables and methods can also be declared with field modifiers. One of these modifiers is 'static', which we have already seen, and which means that there is only one value of the variable for the whole class. Another is 'final', which means that the variable is given an initial value and then cannot be changed. When static and final are used together, the variable is a constant. Static without final indicates a class variable. Final without static indicates that the variable will only be assigned a value once. An assignment to the variable is invalid unless the variable is definitely unassigned immediately prior to the assignment. Usually this means that the assignment is made as part of the declaration of the variable. Using the final modifier for declaring constants is important for program safety and clarity, but also has performance advantages. Methods can also be declared as final, but this facility should be used sparingly: it will constrain the way we can define new classes which extend the current one, as explained later.

Static is also used when we want to declare a class method, and for the special method 'main'. As we saw in Chapter 2, the 'main' method is an entry point to the program and is executed when we invoke the Java virtual machine with the class as argument. In the class Point, as defined above, we have included a simple 'main' method, which can be used to test the other methods of the class. In this case, the method is creating two instances of the class; computing the distance between the two points; and printing the result. The way we create instances of a class is by invoking the 'new' method. Notice that the class does not explicitly define the 'new' method: instead, it defines a constructor with the same arguments. Thus, when we invoke 'new' with two doubles as arguments, a new instance is created and the constructor with the same arguments is invoked to initialise the instance. So p1 is an instance of Point with x = 1.0 and y = 2.0; p2 is an instance of Point with x = 4.0 and y = 6.0. The distance between them is 5.0, being 3.0 in the x direction and 4.0 in the y direction. This value is stored in the variable 'dist'. In the final line of the 'main' method, we are printing out the concatenation of six strings. Although two of the values being concatenated are actually instances of the Point class, when concatenated to strings they are automatically converted to strings using the toString() method. Therefore, what is printed out by the 'main' method is the following:

The distance between 1.0@2.0 and 4.0@6.0 is 5.0

48

## 3.6 Using multiple classes

Now let us consider the class LineSegment, mentioned earlier. A line
segment is defined by its two endpoints, so the class will require two
instance variables to hold references to those points. Suppose that we also
want to be able to control the colour in which a line segment is displayed:
we want all line segments in a picture to be displayed in the same colour,
but that colour can be changed occasionally. We therefore choose to hold
the colour value in a class variable, and we provide a class method to set
the colour to a specified value. For this purpose, we are going to make use
of the class java.awt.Color. Now since that class is not in the same package
as LineSegment, and neither is it in the package java.lang, we need to
explicitly tell the compiler that it is to be used. This is done through the
'import' statement. The definition of the class is as follows:

```
package example.geometric;

import java.awt.Color;

public class LineSegment
{
   private Point endPoint1;
   private Point endPoint2;

   private static Color colour;

   public LineSegment (Point a, Point b)
   {
    endPoint1 = a;
    endPoint2 = b;
   }


   public LineSegment (double x1, double y1, double x2, double y2)
   {
     this (new Point (x1, y1), new Point (x2, y2));
   }

   public double length ()
   {
```

```
    return endPoint1.distanceTo (endPoint2);
  }

  public String toString ()
  {
    return "LineSegment ("+endPoint1+", "+endPoint2+')';
  }

  public static void setColour (Color newColour)
  {
    colour = newColour;
  }

}
```

Notice that, although we need to import the Color class, we are able to use the Point class without importing it. That is because Point is in the same package (example.geometric) whereas Color is in a different package (java.awt). The class variable colour has been declared private, meaning that direct access is allowed only from within the LineSegment class. Public methods will be provided to allow other classes to access the variable indirectly: we have defined a setColour method, and other public methods might be provided if required. We have defined two public constructors for the class. The first one takes two instances of Point as arguments, and creates a line segment between those two points. The second one takes four arguments: the x and y coordinates of each of the two points. The second constructor creates the two points from their coordinates, and then invokes the first constructor. The way to invoke one constructor from another is by using the this() method, with the arguments of the constructor which we wish to invoke. Note that the this() method can only be used within constructors, and has to be the first line of the constructor body. The next method is called length(), and it computes the length of the line segment by finding the distance from one end-point to the other. Since we have already defined a distanceTo() method in the class Point, we make use of that in the definition of length(). To invoke a method on an object of another class, we write the object followed by a dot and the name of the method. The arguments of the method are listed afterwards in parentheses. Since length() is returning the result of distanceTo(), it must have the same return type (double). One thing to be careful of, when invoking a method on another class in this way, is that we must have

50

assigned a value to the object on which we invoke the method. When a variable (such as endPoint1) is declared, it initially has a value of null. If we try to invoke any method on null, we will get a null-pointer exception and the program will fail. In this case, the constructors always assign a value to endPoint1 and endPoint2, so it is safe to invoke distanceTo() on endPoint1. The last method to mention is the toString() method. It is defined in a similar way to the toString() method of the Point class, but the difference here is that the objects to be concatenated include two instances of Point. As we saw with the main method of Point, this is possible because they are automatically converted to strings through the toString() method of the Point class.

### 3.7 Inheritance

Sometimes we may want to create a class B which shares much of the behaviour of an existing class A, but adds some additional features. In such cases, the class B can *extend* class A. That means it inherits all of the data and methods of A, but can also define some additional variables and methods of its own. We call B a *subclass* of A, and A a *superclass* of B. For example, in our definition of the Point class, the coordinates of the point are set in the constructor and there is no mechanism provided to change them. If we want to move the point to a different position, we need to create a new instance of Point. This is reasonable as a general policy, but perhaps there will be situations in which we really want to change the position of an existing point. To allow this, we can create a subclass of Point, which we shall call MobilePoint. The subclass will be just like the original class, but will additionally allow us to modify the coordinates.

```
package example.geometric;

public class MobilePoint extends Point
{

    public MobilePoint (double xVal, double yVal)
    {
    super (xVal, yVal);
    }
```

```
public void moveTo (double newX, double newY)
   {
     x = newX;
     y = newY;
   }

   public static void main (String[] args)
   {
     MobilePoint mp = new MobilePoint (1.0, 2.0);
     Point p = new Point (1.0, 2.0);
     mp.moveTo (13.0, 7.0);
     System.out.println ("The mobile point is now located at " + mp);
     System.out.println ("The distance between " + mp + " and " + p + " is "
       + dist);
   }

}
```

The declaration 'MobilePoint extends Point' means that the class
MobilePoint will inherit all the variables and methods of the class Point.
Thus, anything which can be done to an instance of Point can also be done
to an instance of MobilePoint, with the following proviso: methods defined
in the subclass (MobilePoint) are not allowed to access variables or
methods which are declared as private in the superclass (Point). This is
why, when we declared the class Point, we needed to declare x and y to be
protected rather than private. Had they been private, they would have been
hidden from the subclass MobilePoint. As it is, we are able to access them
in the method moveTo. Note that in Java it is not possible to allow a
variable to be accessed only from subclasses: by making the variables
protected, we are allowing access from any class in the package (subclass
or not), and to subclasses which may be defined in different packages.

In this example we want to define the constructor for MobilePoint to work
in the same way as that for Point. Therefore, the constructor simply invokes
the constructor of the superclass. The way to do that in Java is by using the
super() method. This method (similar to this()) is used only in constructors,
and only in the first line of the body of the constructor. Its meaning is to
invoke the constructor in the superclass with the arguments given to
super(). These are not necessarily the same as the arguments of the
constructor of the subclass, though in this example they are the same. For

52

example, if the subclass had introduced an additional instance variable, we might add an extra argument to the constructor for MobilePoint. That extra argument could then be used in the constructor of MobilePoint to initialise the additional instance variable: but such initialisation must be done after the call to the constructor of the superclass.

The main() method of MobilePoint creates a mobile point, and then creates a point at the same position. The mobile point is then moved to a new position, and its distance from the fixed point is computed. The output of this method is as follows:

The mobile point is now located at 13.0@7.0
The distance between the points is 13.0

When we define a new class in Java, it always extends some existing class. By default, if we do not specify a superclass explicitly, it will extend java.lang.Object. That class is the root of the Java class hierarchy, and defines some basic behaviour which applies to all classes. When we extend a class, there may be some behaviour which we do not wish to inherit exactly: rather, we would prefer for our new class to implement a particular method in a slightly different way. This can be accomplished by *overriding* that method in the new class. To override a method, we simply define a new method in the subclass with the same name, such that the parameters match in both number and type. In that case, the method in the superclass is not available to the subclass. In the event of the method in the subclass having a different number of parameters, or any of those parameters having different type from the corresponding parameter in the superclass's method, the method is instead *overloaded*. That means that the subclass can access two methods of the same name: the one which is invoked is determined by the number and type of the parameters in the invocation.

Inheritance of static variables and methods is different from their non-static counterparts. A static variable defined in the superclass is accessible from the subclass: however, it is quite possible for the subclass to define an entirely different variable with the same name (this variable may or may not have the same type as the one in the superclass). In that case the variable in the superclass is said to be hidden from the subclass, because a reference to the variable from the subclass will be taken to mean the one defined in that class. For example, suppose we add the following line to the definition of the class Point:

static char displaySymbol = '+'; // symbol to use when displaying a point

If we want to use a different symbol for displaying mobile points, we might define another variable in the class MobilePoint:

static char displaySymbol = 'x'; // the symbol for displaying mobile points

Now let us add the following line to the main() method of MobilePoint:

System.out.println ("The display symbol is " + displaySymbol);

The output produced by the above line of code will be:

The display symbol is x

Note that, if we had not defined displaySymbol in MobilePoint, the statement would have referred instead to the displaySymbol defined in Point, and the following would have been output:

The display symbol is +

As it is, the variable in Point is hidden from MobilePoint, but it can still be accessed if required by using the notation Point.displaySymbol. Thus,

System.out.println ("The display symbols are " + displaySymbol + " and " + Point.displaySymbol);

This redefining of a variable in the subclass gives us the ability to define what in Smalltalk are called class instance variables: that is, a variable whose value can be different in each subclass. That is really the only circumstance in which we might sensibly wish to hide the variable in the superclass by redefining it in the subclass. In any other circumstances, it is better to avoid using the same name for variables in the subclass and superclass.

Constructors, unlike methods, are not inherited by subclasses. Instead, the following rules apply:
- If no constructor is explicitly defined for a class, the compiler will add a constructor with no arguments and an empty body.

54

- In any constructor which does not begin with a call to super(), with or without arguments, the compiler will automatically add a call to super() with no arguments.

The effect of these rules is such that it can sometimes look as though constructors are being inherited. However, there are significant differences. If the subclass does not define any constructors, it will get a no-argument constructor which is just like that of its superclass: but if the superclass includes any constructors with arguments, the subclass will not be given any similar constructor. And if the subclass defines a constructor with arguments, it will not get a no-argument constructor at all unless it defines one explicitly. For example, the class MobilePoint as defined above has a constructor with two arguments. The compiler therefore will not add any further constructors to the class.

### 3.8 Abstract classes

In the previous example, we were able to create instances of both subclass (MobilePoint) and superclass (Point). There are times, however, when we want to define a superclass for which no instances can be created. In that case, the superclass exists only to provide some shared variables and methods which can be inherited by all of its subclasses. We call such a superclass an *abstract class*. A class for which instances can be created is called a *concrete class*.

As an example, let us suppose that we wish to define classes Circle and Polygon as subclasses of an abstract class called Figure. We can declare the class Figure by including the 'abstract' keyword:

```
public abstract class Figure
{
  // any variables or methods defined here
}
```

The keyword 'abstract' means that no instances of the class can be created. If we try to create an instance using

Figure newFig = new Figure();

the compiler will generate an error.

An abstract class (unlike a concrete class) is allowed to define abstract methods. An abstract method contains only a signature, not a body. Its purpose is to state that every concrete subclass must provide an implementation for the abstract method. For example, we might wish to find the area of a figure. The method of computing the area of a polygon will be quite different from that for a circle, so each will need to provide a separate implementation. Nevertheless, the abstract class can indicate that the method is available:

```
package example.geometric;

public abstract class Figure
{
  public abstract double area();
}
```

Now in the definition of Circle, we provide an implementation for the method (note that the java.lang.Math class provides a value for $\pi$, the ratio between the circumference and diameter of a circle):

```
package example.geometric;

public class Circle extends Figure
{
  private double radius;
  private Point centre;

  public Circle (Point c, double r)
  {
    centre = c;
    radius = r;
  }

  public double area()
  {
    return Math.PI * radius * radius;
  }
}
```

Knowing that every concrete subclass must implement the method means that we can invoke the method on a figure without even knowing the subclass to which it belongs. Java will select the appropriate implementation at runtime, depending on the class of the object in question. For example, let us consider the following code snippet:

```
Figure fig = null;
// .......
// some code here to assign a non-null value to fig
// .......
double area = fig.area();
```

This code will compile, because the area() method has been defined in the Figure class. But it is not clear at compile time which implementation of area() needs to be invoked, because we don't know the subclass to which fig belongs. Indeed, the subclass might depend on user input. We have made use of a feature known as polymorphism, or dynamic binding, about which we shall expand below.

Inheritance is useful because it allows us to reuse existing code which is already known to be reliable, thus speeding application development and making the code more reliable. On the other hand, proper use of inheritance requires a lot of care. Subclasses inherit all of the data and behaviour of the superclasses. Inheritance therefore should not be used when only some of the data or behaviour applies to the subclass.

Inheritance is widely used throughout the JDK, for example in the Number hierarchy. The abstract class java.lang.Number defines various abstract methods which its concrete subclasses are required to implement. Those subclasses (such as Integer, Long, Short, Byte, Float and Double) must each define a translation of their value to int, long, short, byte, float and double.

### 3.9 Polymorphism

As the application is developed, the class Figure may be expanded with some variables and concrete methods. Up to now, however, we have only defined an abstract method for it. In practice, we would not create a class containing nothing but abstract methods. Such a class can have no instances, and provides no common behaviour for its subclasses. Those subclasses, indeed, will have nothing in common except for a shared requirement to implement one or more methods which have been declared abstract in the superclass. In these circumstances, there would be no need to declare the abstract class Figure. Instead, we can declare an *interface* which specifies the methods to be implemented. Thus

```
public interface GeoFigure
{
  public double area();
}
```

Methods defined in an interface are implicitly abstract, but do not need to be explicitly defined as such. An interface may also contain definitions of constants, which are implicitly public, static and final: but again the modifiers can be omitted from the declaration of the interface. An interface has several things in common with a class, but there are also a number of differences between the two. The similarities are:

- Each is usually defined in its own source file, and compiled into its own class file
- Each is defined with an access modifier
- One interface may extend another, just as one class may extend another
- Both interfaces and classes are valid types which can be used in variable declarations (more about this later)

The differences include the following:

- An interface can include constants, but cannot include variables
- An interface includes only method signatures, not method bodies
- We cannot create instances of interfaces, only of classes
- A class may *extend* another class; a class may *implement* one or more interfaces
- An interface may extend more than one other interface

To illustrate the penultimate point above, the definition of the class Circle might be rewritten in the following way:

```
package example.geometric;
```

```java
public class Circle implements GeoFigure
{
    private double radius;
    private Point centre;

    public Circle (Point c, double r)
    {
        centre = c;
        radius = r;
    }

    public double area()
    {
        return Math.PI * radius * radius;
    }

    public static void main (String[] args)
    {
        Point ctr = new Point (0.0, 3.0);
        GeoFigure gf = new Circle (ctr, 1.0);
        double a = gf.area();
        System.out.println ("The area of the figure is " + a);
    }

}
```

The main() method illustrates the use of an interface as type for the variable gf. In this instance, we can see that the variable will always be assigned a value which is an instance of Circle. In general, though, it can happen that the class of a variable is dependent on input data. When a method is invoked on a variable whose type is an interface, the implementation of the method is chosen at runtime. Thus, interfaces provide us with a means to support polymorphism.

If inheritance is sometimes overused, polymorphism is a concept which is often overlooked or under-used. It allows us to define two classes which implement the same interface, even though they may not inherit any common data or behaviour from each other or from any third class. It requires more development effort to create the classes, because each must be built from scratch, but its great advantage is that it allows client classes to be written in such a way that they can make use of any class which implements the interface. For example, if we were to write a method to sort objects, it really would not matter which class those objects belonged to. All that we would require is that we can compare any one with any other, and determine their ordering. Polymorphism is also invaluable for supporting access to external systems such as databases. Database systems such as Oracle, DB2 and SQL Server are all implemented in quite different ways, yet they can all be accessed from Java in the same way. This is because they all support the JDBC interfaces which we shall discuss later in the book.

## 3.10 Exception handling

In procedural languages, it is common for functions to return an error code when an unexpected condition arises. Thus, for example, the function might return a result of zero when execution completes as expected, and a negative result when something went wrong. The precise value of the negative result may depend on the nature of the error. The calling function needs to check the result, and take appropriate action accordingly. Object-oriented languages take a different approach. The default assumption is that processing succeeded as expected. If something went wrong, the method will throw an exception. Again, there can be many different types of exception, representing different types of underlying problem. The calling method can catch particular types of exception, and take action appropriate to that exception type. Any exception which it does not catch will automatically be thrown to the method which invoked it. Exceptions may be passed as far up the calling stack as desired, but it is important to catch them at some point. If an exception is left uncaught, it will be displayed to the user in an inappropriate format.

Exceptions fall into three main categories: declared exceptions, runtime exceptions and errors. Declared exceptions are thrown by methods, which need to declare which exceptions they can throw. In this way, a calling method knows which exceptions can be thrown, and can decide which ones to catch and which ones to throw to its calling methods. Runtime exceptions (null pointers, array index out of bounds, class cast errors, etc) are usually caused by programming mistakes. They do not need to be declared: instead, we should try to develop code in such a way that they do

60

not arise (for example, if there is a possibility that a variable has value null, we should check for a null value before invoking a method on that variable). Finally, errors (such as out of memory errors) are indicative of serious problems which the application should not try to catch. They should occur relatively infrequently.

An example of a method with a declared exception is the class method parseInt(String) in the class java.lang.Integer. This method receives a string as input, and converts it to an int: but it can only do that if the string does represent a valid integer. If instead a string such as "Hello World" is passed in, it will throw a NumberFormatException. Thus the method signature is

public static int parseInt (String aString) throws NumberFormatException

Now let us suppose that we require a method which will read a number from standard input and return that value as result. We might write the method as follows:

```
public int getInt ()
{
    String val = null;
    int intVal;
    boolean readOK = false;
    while (! readOK)
    {
        try
        {
            byte[] buf = new byte[10];
            System.out.print ("Enter an integer: ");
            System.in.read (buf);
            val = new String (buf);
            intVal = Integer.parseInt (val);
            readOK = true;
        }
        catch (NumberFormatException e)
        {
            readOK = false; // repeat the loop
        }
    }
    return intVal;
```

}

Exceptions are handled by writing try/catch blocks, the general form of which is as follows:

```
try
{
    // define steps for normal execution flow
}
catch (SomeException e)
{
    // define steps for handling exceptions of type SomeException
}
.....
catch (SomeOtherException ex)
{
    // define steps for handling exceptions of type SomeOtherException
}
finally
{
    // define steps for general tidying up
}
```

The try block is executed and, if it completes successfully, processing continues from the statement following the try-catch-finally statement. In the event of an exception being thrown during processing of the try block, control immediately transfers to the appropriate catch block, according to the type of the exception. Thus in the getInt() example above, we can be sure that after each iteration of the loop, readOK will be true if processing completed successfully and false if an exception was thrown. Hence the loop is repeated, prompting for more input, until the input can be processed successfully.

In general, each try block must have either one or more catch blocks or a finally block (frequently, it will have both catch and finally). The difference between catch and finally is that the catch block exists only to catch specific exceptions, and it is executed only in the event of such an exception being thrown. The finally block, if present, is always executed at the end of the try-catch, regardless of whether or not an exception was thrown. The finally block is useful for ensuring that resources are released when they are no longer needed, a topic which we shall cover in Section 4.2.

## 3.11 Garbage collection

One of the advantages of Java over C++ is that it makes memory management much easier. Rather than the programmer having responsibility for deleting objects when they are no longer needed, Java provides automatic garbage collection which runs periodically to identify objects whose memory space can be reclaimed.

Garbage collection was originally developed for LISP in the 1950s, and subsequently used by Smalltalk and then by Java. It works by maintaining a reference count for each object, i.e., the number of variables which refer to the object. As soon as the reference count becomes zero, the object is garbage and the space can be reclaimed. Let us consider a simple example:

```
String a = new String ("String1");
a = new String ("String2");
```

The first line creates a new object of type String, with a reference count of 1 (the variable a refers to it). The second line creates another new object, also with a reference count of 1. This statement also reduces the reference count of the first object to zero, because a no longer refers to it.

Reassigning a variable is one way of reducing the reference count. Another way is for the variable to go out of scope. Consider the following block which declares a local variable:

```
{
    String s = new String ("A String");
    // do some more processing here
}
// s is now out of scope
```

When the program leaves the block, the variable s becomes out of scope. This decrements the reference count of the object to which it refers. Unless there is another variable, one which is still in scope, which refers to that object, it will be available for garbage collection.

Garbage collection runs as a low-priority background process. In general, we cannot be sure when it will run. So making an object available for garbage collection does not guarantee that it will be immediately reclaimed. There is a method on the java.lang.System class,

System.gc()

which suggests to the virtual machine that garbage collection should be run. However, even this does not guarantee that the garbage collector will definitely be run at that time. Therefore it is best to assume that your program will use rather more memory than would be the case if all garbage was immediately removed. You can allocate additional memory when starting up the virtual machine:

java –Xms 512M –Xmx1024M MyClass

The –ms flag is used to specify the amount of memory to allocate initially to the virtual machine, and the –mx flag is used to specify the maximum memory to allow. The above example therefore allocates an initial 512Mbytes, but allows an extra 512Mbytes to be claimed if needed.

65

# Chapter 4

# COLLECTIONS, FILES AND THREADS

---

In this chapter, we shall look at some additional features provided by Java. Specifically, the collections framework which allows for programming with a wide range of data structures; the use of files for input and output of data; and the creation of multiple concurrent threads within a program.

## 4.1 Collections

We have already seen how arrays can be used in Java to group a collection of values into a single variable. The array is an important feature of the language, but it is by no means the only way of defining a collection. In particular, the array has a major limitation in that once it has been created it is not possible to add or remove an element. Besides this, array elements can only be accessed by their index: depending on the circumstances, this may or may not be a convenient way of accessing data. Accordingly, Java provides a collections framework which supports a range of different types of collection, each of which is useful in particular situations.

The collections framework consists of a set of interfaces, and classes which implement those interfaces. The classes provide both the data structures and the algorithms which act upon those data structures. A feature of the collections is that the algorithms can be written independently of the type of object held within the collections. Thus, it does not matter whether we are dealing with a collection of apples or a collection of oranges: the operations on that collection are the same.

An important concept for dealing with collections is the idea of an *iterator*. An iterator allows us to loop over all of the items within a collection, and is an idea which is very frequently used. Iterators can loop over the elements either in non-deterministic order or using the natural ordering of elements within the collection.

The interfaces and classes of the collections framework are held within the package java.util. The most fundamental interface is java.util.Collection, which defines methods to return the number of elements in a collection; to check whether a given object is an element of the collection; to convert the collection to an array containing the same elements; and various other operations which apply to collections of all kinds. Inheriting from this interface, there are three sub-interfaces which describe more specific types of collection:
- List, for defining an ordered collection of elements, which may include duplicates
- Set, for defining a collection without duplicates
- Queue, in JDK 1.5 and later, for defining specific operations on a queue
The interface java.util.Set represents, by default, an unordered set. In cases where ordering is significant, a sub-interface called java.util.SortedSet is provided.

You may have noticed that List and Set cover between them only three out of four possible cases. If we want ordering and duplicates, we use a List; if we want ordering but no duplicates, we use a SortedSet; and if we want neither ordering nor duplicates, we use a Set. But what if we want to allow duplicates but no ordering (what is commonly known as a Bag) ? Java does not explicitly provide support for bags within the collections framework, but it does provide a more general interface which can be used to implement a bag. Recall that a bag is defined not by any ordering of its elements, but merely by the number of times each element occurs. It can be represented, therefore, by a set of associations which link each element to the number of times it occurs in the bag. This is made possible by the interface java.util.Map. The Map interface is not a sub-interface of Collection, but is part of a separate hierarchy. In general, a Map is a set of associations which associate values of one type with keys of another class. In the case of a bag, the keys are the elements of the bag, and the values are the number of instances of each of those elements.

Java provides a number of implementations for each of the interfaces in the collections framework. When programming with collections, we need to decide which implementation to use when we *create* the collection; the rest of the time, though, it is best to think in terms of interfaces rather than implementations. By writing the program in terms of interfaces, we achieve two main advantages:

- If we decide at some later date to change the implementation, we only need to change the statement which creates the collection
- If the program is divided into several methods, and only one of those methods creates the collection, all the other methods are potentially reusable by other applications which might choose a different implementation for the collection

When creating a collection which will not allow duplicates, the usual implementation is java.util.HashSet. The HashSet provides a fast implementation based on hashing, which can quickly locate an element within the set. Its one disadvantage is that it maintains a rather arbitrary ordering of the elements. In cases where you may want to iterate over the elements in a particular order, it may be preferable to use java.util.TreeSet, which implements the SortedSet interface but is much slower. A third implementation, java.util.LinkedHashSet, is a compromise between the two. It uses hashing to obtain an efficient implementation, but also links the elements to allow sequential access when required.

When creating a collection which allows both duplicates and ordering, the usual implementation is provided by java.util.ArrayList. An ArrayList is essentially a resizeable array: it allows access by index or iteration, similar to an array, but also allows new elements to be added. The most efficient way to add an element is to place it at the end of the list. Insertion or deletion of interior elements requires adjustment of the indices of other elements, and is consequently slower. An alternative implementation, java.util.LinkedList, is good for iterating and deleting internal elements and for adding to the beginning. LinkedList also implements the Queue interface of JDK 1.5.

The options for implementing a Map are similar to those for a Set. The usual implementation is HashMap, which is fast but has an unpredictable order of iteration. TreeMap implements SortedMap and gives key-ordered iteration. LinkedHashMap gives insertion-order iteration and is nearly as fast as HashMap.

Let us now look at an example. Suppose we have a collection of words, and we want to know how many of the words have ten or more letters. We can use an iterator to examine each of the words in the collection, and test the length of each word. The following method can be used:

```
public int longWordCount (Collection wordCollection)
{
    int longWords = 0;
    Iterator it = wordCollection.iterator();
    while (it.hasNext())
    {
        String nextWord = (String)it.next();
        if (nextWord.length() >= 10)
            ++longWords;
    }
    return longWords;
}
```

We obtain an iterator by using the iterator() method of the Collection interface. The iterator has a hasNext() method to check whether there are any more elements in the collection, and a next() method to get the next element. The looping construct, in which we first test for the existence of another element and then fetch it, is a very common approach when using iterators. Notice also that, having obtained the next element, we have cast it to an instance of String. In order that we can test the length of the string, it is necessary to know that it is a string. Yet, in general, a collection can contain instances of any class.

The approach illustrated above is the one taken when using JDK 1.4 or earlier. Because a collection contains instances of Object, it is usually necessary to cast elements to their actual class when they are extracted from the collection. This puts the onus on the programmer to know the class to which elements belong. If the programmer forgets, or mistakenly adds an instance of a different class to the collection, the program will fail with a ClassCastException at runtime. Moreover, if a decision is taken to change the element type of a collection, it is necessary to find all the places where a class cast is made and correct them. Because of these problems, a decision was taken in JDK 1.5 to allow the element type of a collection to be declared. Thus in our example, we can (in JDK 1.5) declare that we are

69

working with a collection of strings. This allows us to extract a string from the collection without the need for a cast. Thus,

```
public int longWordCount (Collection<String> wordCollection)
{
    int longWords = 0;
    Iterator<String> it = wordCollection.iterator();
    while (it.hasNext())
    {
        String nextWord = it.next();
        if (nextWord.length() >= 10)
            ++longWords;
    }
    return longWords;
}
```

Another option in JDK 1.5 is to use the for-each loop. This avoids the use of iterators at all. The above method could be rewritten as follows:

```
public int longWordCount (Collection<String> wordCollection)
{
    int longWords = 0;
    for (String w: wordCollection)
        if (w.length() >= 10)
            ++longWords;
    return longWords;
}
```

This last form of the method is both simpler and safer than the original one, though the original approach is still required if using JDK 1.4.

Let us now look at some programming examples in which we need to create a collection, and consequently need to choose the most appropriate kind of collection for the circumstances. In the first example, we are going to take a collection of strings (each assumed to represent a single word) and note which letters appear as the first letter of one or more of the words. We are not interested in how many of the words begin with a given letter, only that there is at least one such word. Therefore we choose a Set as the most appropriate interface for holding the collection of letters found. With a Set, we can just add elements without checking for duplicates. The implementations of the Set interface ensure that no Set can contain two elements a and b such that a.equals(b), or two null values. Having chosen the interface, we next need to decide which implementation of the interface to use. In this case, we are going to use a HashSet because it is the most efficient implementation and we are not concerned about obtaining the letters in a particular order (if we wanted to display the letters in alphabetical order, we might prefer one of the other implementations). The method which derives the set of first letters is quite straightforward. We iterate over the collection of words, obtain the first letter of each word, and add the letter to the set. At the end, we return the set as the result of the method. To obtain the first character of a string, we use the method charAt(), with an index of zero. Note that this method returns a char, which is not an object. Only first-class objects can be added to collections so, at least in Java 1.4, we need to create an instance of the wrapper class Character before adding to the Set. The complete code for the method is listed below:

```
public Set firstLetters (Collection words)
{
    Set startingLetters = new HashSet();
    Iterator it = words.iterator();
    while (it.hasNext())
    {
        String nextWord = (String)it.next();
        Character firstLetter = new Character(nextWord.charAt(0));
        startingLetters.add(firstLetter);
    }
    return startingLetters;
}
```

For our second example, we modify the requirement slightly so that, as well as finding which letters appear as the first letter of a word, we also want to know how many of the words begin with a given letter. This requirement makes the Map interface the most appropriate. We can use a map in which the keys are the letters and the values are the number of occurrences of those letters. The general structure of the method will be similar to the previous example, but the process of adding to the map is more complicated. Before adding a letter to the map, we need to check whether that letter already occurs as a key in the map. If it does, we need to increment the associated value. If the key is not already present, we add it with an associated value of one. The code for this method is shown below:

```
public Map letterCounts (Collection words)
{
    Map counts = new HashMap();
    Iterator it = words.iterator();
    while (it.hasNext())
    {
        String nextWord = (String)it.next();
        Character firstLetter = new Character(nextWord.charAt(0));
        if (counts.containsKey(firstLetter))
        {
            Integer count = (Integer)counts.get(firstLetter);
            counts.put(firstLetter, new Integer(1 + count.intValue()));
        }
        else
            counts.put (firstLetter, new Integer(1));
    }
    return counts;
}
```

Just as a Set prevents duplicate values being added, so a map prevents duplicate keys from being added. So the put() method can be used both to add a new key and to replace the value associated with an existing key.

Both of the above examples were written using the style of JDK 1.4. There are several features of the methods which are somewhat unsatisfactory, and where the code can be significantly simplified using the newer features of JDK 1.5. Consider the following:

- In the first example, we wanted to add a char to a Set but had to create an instance of Character before adding the element. In the second example, we wanted to add a char as key and an int as value, but needed to convert both to objects. We also needed to obtain the value from an Integer in order to perform arithmetic on it. JDK 1.5 simplifies the coding by allowing us to add primitive values to a collection and to perform arithmetic directly on objects, through a feature known as autoboxing and unboxing. This means that the conversion is done for you behind the scenes, and code is kept simple and clear.

- Each of the examples used an iterator to iterate over the collection. Using JDK 1.5, we would instead use the for-each loop as described earlier.
- The return types of the methods have been declared as Set and Map. A client class which invokes the methods will need to know that the first method returns a set of characters and the second method returns a map which associates characters to integers. When it extracts elements, it will need to cast them appropriately, and a ClassCastException will be thrown if it casts to the wrong type. In JDK 1.5, we would declare the return types as Set<Character> and Map<Character,Integer>, respectively. This allows the compiler to do type checking, so that only elements of the correct type can be added to a collection, and client classes can extract elements of the correct type without casting.

## 4.2 Files

In Chapter 2, we introduced very simple mechanisms for inputting data to a program. Those mechanisms are sufficient for only the simplest cases, where a few simple values need to be provided. When a program needs to handle substantial volumes of data, it is necessary to use either files or a database. In this section, we look at the most important classes which Java provides for accessing files.

There are two main types of file. A binary file stores each byte in the same way that would be represented in memory. This makes for efficient reading and writing of large files, and is typically used for storing image data such as maps and photographs. A text file stores data as characters, and requires conversion when data are transferred between file and memory. A text file is less efficient, but is human-readable and therefore convenient for storing business data such as numbers and strings.

The classes which support file access are found in the package java.io. The most important of those classes are the following:
- File, which represents file and directory path names and supports operations to create or delete a file or directory, and list the files in a directory.
- FileInputStream, which supports reading of bytes from a binary file.
- FileOutputStream, which supports writing of bytes to a binary file.

- FileReader, which can read bytes from a text file and convert to characters.
- BufferedReader, which provides a wrapper to support buffering and hence more efficient reading of text files; it also provides a method for reading a line of text from a file.
- FileWriter, which can write characters (or a String) to a text file.
- BufferedWriter, which provides the wrapper to support buffered writes to a text file.
- PrintWriter, which supports writing of objects to a text file, using the string representation of the object. The string representation of an object obj is derived via String.valueOf(obj). This is equivalent to obj.toString() except that it will convert a null value to the string "null" instead of throwing a null pointer exception.

In this section, we shall look at three commonly-used operations: reading numbers from a text file, reading records from a text file and reading/writing a binary file.

### 4.2.1 Reading numbers from a text file

Let us suppose that we are reading data from a text file which is known to contain only numbers. We create a FileReader, and wrap a BufferedReader around it for efficiency. Now, rather than read a character at a time, we would like to read a number at a time. This is made possible by a class called StreamTokenizer which is useful for precisely this kind of situation. StreamTokenizer can be used to identify either numbers or words in a stream, by parsing the input stream. All that is needed is a simple loop in which we repeatedly get the next token (number, in this case) from the input stream. The tokenizer holds the token value in a public field called nval. Reading stops when the end of file is reached. The method below, being just for illustrative purposes, simply prints out the values as they are read. In practice, we might want a method of this kind to add the numbers to a collection, or do some other processing.

```
public void content (File f)
{
    try
    {
        Reader r = new BufferedReader (new FileReader (f));
```

```
            StreamTokenizer st = new StreamTokenizer (r);
            st.parseNumbers();
            st.nextToken();
            while (st.ttype != StreamTokenizer.TT_EOF)
            {
                System.out.println ("Read: "+st.nval);
                st.nextToken();
            }
        }
        catch (FileNotFoundException e1)
        {
            System.out.println ("The specified file "+f.getName()+
                                " does not exist");
        }
        catch (IOException e2)
        {
            e2.printStackTrace();
        }
        finally
        {
            try
            {
                rdr.close();
                System.out.println ("Closed file");
            }
            catch (Exception ex)
            {
                System.out.println ("Failed to close file");
            }
        }
    }
```

One of the tricky aspects of file processing is the handling of exceptions. If we try to open a file which does exist, or for which we do not have authorisation, a FileNotFoundException will be thrown. If a read operation fails for some reason, an IOException will be thrown. A method which does file processing will have to either handle these exceptions or else throw them and let its client classes decide how to handle them. If the exceptions are handled, the minimum that should be done is to write out a message so that it is clear why the processing failed. For debugging, it is

75

useful to print out the stack trace in order to locate the source of the problem. In this case, for illustration, we have chosen to handle the FileNotFoundException by printing out a message that the file does not exist. In the case of the IOException, we have chosen to print out the stack trace. The finally clause is a good place to close the file, but note that closing a file can also throw an exception: hence the file close operation is done within another try-catch block.

## 4.2.2 Reading records from a text file

More commonly, the requirement is to read a file of records rather than a file containing only numbers. Our next example is a method to read records from a file, where the assumption is that each record occupies one line of the file. We are going to read each field as a string: if there is a need to convert some fields to other types, that processing could be added to the method. Again, as it is just for illustrative purposes, we shall simply print out the values as they are read. The method makes use of the readLine() method of BufferedReader, to read a complete record at a time. It then invokes another method to process the record and divide it into its constituent fields. The process of identifying constituent fields is handled by the class java.util.StringTokenizer, which is quite similar to StreamTokenizer but works on a string rather than a stream.

```
//import java.util.StringTokenizer;

private void processRecord (String nextLine)
{
    StringTokenizer st = new StringTokenizer (nextLine);
    while (st.hasMoreTokens())
    {
        String nextTok = st.nextToken();
        System.out.println ("\tGot field: "+nextTok);
    }
}

public void readRecords (File f)
{
```

```
BufferedReader rdr = null;
try
{
    rdr = new BufferedReader (new FileReader (f));
    String nextLine = rdr.readLine();
    while (nextLine != null)
    {
        System.out.println ("Got record:");
      processRecord (nextLine);
      nextLine = rdr.readLine();
    }
}
catch (FileNotFoundException e1)
{
    System.out.println ("The specified file "+f.getName()+
        " does not exist");
}
catch (IOException e2)
{
    e2.printStackTrace();
}
finally
{
    try
    {
        rdr.close();
        System.out.println ("Closed file");
    }
    catch (Exception ex)
    {
        System.out.println ("Failed to close file");
    }
}
}
```

The method separates the fields of the different records by indenting the display of the fields. The tab character (\t) is printed at the start of the output of each field.

### 4.2.3 Reading and writing Binary files

The mechanisms for reading and writing binary files are quite different from those for reading and writing text files. In some ways it is simpler, because we are transferring bytes directly between file and memory. The class FileInputStream provides methods to read from a binary file into a byte array, and to write from a byte array to a file. The main issue to deal with then is that the file may be large, so we want to read/write the file in chunks rather than doing the whole thing in a single operation.

To read a binary file, we shall define a chunk size of 1024 bytes for this example. We shall read the first 1024 bytes into the array, then save a copy of that array and read the next 1024 bytes. We then concatenate the two arrays. The class java.lang.System provides an arraycopy method which can be used to implement the concatenation efficiently. Note that when the last chunk is read, it is likely to contain fewer than 1024 bytes. To handle this eventuality, we need to make use of the value returned by the read() method, which indicates how many bytes were actually read. The code for the readFile() method is shown below:

```
public static final int BUF_SIZE = 1024;

public byte[] readFile (File f)
{
    byte[] result = new byte[0];
    int totalBytes = 0;
    FileInputStream str = null;
    try
    {
        str = new FileInputStream(f);
        byte[] buf = new byte[BUF_SIZE];
        int numRead = str.read(buf);
        while (numRead > 0)
        {
            byte[] oldResult = result;
            result = new byte[oldResult.length+numRead];
            System.arraycopy(oldResult,0,result,0,oldResult.length);
            System.arraycopy(buf,0,result,oldResult.length,numRead);
            numRead = str.read(buf);
```

```
            }
         return result;
      }
      catch (FileNotFoundException e1)
      {
         System.out.println ("The specified file "+f.getName()+
                              " does not exist");
         return null;
      }
      catch (IOException e2)
      {
         e2.printStackTrace();
         return null;
      }
      finally
      {
         try
         {
            if (str != null)
               str.close();
            System.out.println ("File closed");
         }
         catch (Exception ex)
         {
            System.out.println ("Failed to close file");
         }
      }
   }
}
```

The mechanism for writing the file is a little simpler than that for reading.
We can still write the file in chunks, but the process of identifying the next
chunk involves nothing more than incrementing the array index. The
number of bytes to be written is known: although the final chunk is likely to
be smaller, this can be easily identified by comparing the array index with
the length of the array being written.

```
public void writeFile (byte[] contents, File dest)
{
    FileOutputStream str = null;
    try
    {
        str = new FileOutputStream(dest);
        int startIndex = 0;
        while (startIndex < contents.length)
        {
            int chunkSize = Math.min(BUF_SIZE,contents.length-
            startIndex);
            str.write(contents, startIndex, chunkSize);
            startIndex += chunkSize;
        }
    }
    catch (FileNotFoundException e1)
    {
        System.out.println ("The specified file "+dest.getName()+
                        " could not be opened");
    }
    catch (IOException e2)
    {
        e2.printStackTrace();
    }
    finally
    {
        try
        {
            if (str != null)
                str.close();
            System.out.println ("File closed");
        }
        catch (Exception ex)
        {
            System.out.println ("Failed to close file");
        }
    }
}
```

## 4.3 Threads

Complex programs often require multiple threads to execute concurrently. For example, a server which needs to handle requests from multiple clients will typically use a separate thread for each concurrent request. In that way, it is not necessary to wait for one request to complete before beginning the next one.

A Java thread is a lightweight process which can be created during the execution of a Java program. There are two ways of creating a thread:
1) Create an instance of a class which is a subclass of java.lang.Thread, using Thread myThread = new MyThread();
2) Create an instance of a class which implements the interface java.lang.Runnable, using
   Thread myThread = new Thread (new MyRunnable());

The second approach is usually preferred. It is more general, and more appropriate to most circumstances since we are usually creating not a special kind of thread but a special kind of object to run in a thread.

At a given time, a thread is in one of the following states:
- *New Thread*, meaning that it has been created but has not been started
- *Runnable*, which means that it is available to run. There may be several threads which are in the Runnable state at a given time, in which case it is the responsibility of the scheduler to decide which of them to run
- *Not Runnable*, which means that it has started but is currently waiting for some event to occur before it is available to run again. It may be waiting for some resource, or it may have suspended itself temporarily.
- *Dead*, which means that execution of the thread has completed

In the remainder of this section, we shall look in some detail at how a thread can move from one state to another.

When a thread is first created, it is a New Thread. It becomes Runnable when its start() method is invoked. Thus,

Thread myThread = new Thread (new MyRunnable());
myThread.start();

The start() method allocates resources to the thread and invokes the run() method. If you subclass Thread, you need to implement run() in your subclass; if you define a class which implements Runnable (as in the example above) you need to implement run() in that class. Note, however, that the run() method will not necessarily be executed immediately if there are other competing threads in the Runnable state. The scheduler will decide when to run each thread, so the behaviour of a multi-threaded program is non-deterministic in general.

The non-deterministic scheduling of threads may not be a problem if the threads are carrying out independent tasks. It can be a problem, though, if they are accessing shared resources. Consider the following method:

```
public int getSequenceNumber()
{
    ++counter;
    return counter;
}
```

Such a method might be used to obtain unique identifiers. But suppose there are two different threads which want to execute that method at about the same time. There would then be the possibility of erroneous results, for example as a result of the following sequence of operations:
1)  Thread-1 increments counter
2)  Thread-2 increments counter
3)  Thread-1 reads counter and returns value
4)  Thread-2 reads counter and returns value
Suppose the counter initially had a value of zero. Then both threads would return a value of 2, so the desired behaviour of generating unique identifiers would be lost. The problem with the above sequence of operations is, of course, that Thread-2 started to execute the method before Thread-1 had finished executing it. What is needed is a mechanism which will guarantee that the method getSequenceNumber() is executed as an atomic operation. This is achieved via the concept of a monitor lock. In Java, each object has a monitor which holds a lock, and a thread can obtain the lock in order to execute an atomic operation on the object. When the thread has completed execution of the operation, it will release the lock so that other threads can access the object. It is not necessary to obtain a lock for every operation on every object, only for those operations where there is potential for conflict. In Java, we use the keyword *synchronized* to indicate that a monitor lock needs to be obtained. A synchronized static method requires the monitor lock on the class, while a non-static synchronized method requires the monitor lock only on the instance. Thus,

```
public synchronized int getSequenceNumber()
{
    ++counter;
    return counter;
}
```

By specifying that the method is synchronized, we force a thread to obtain the monitor lock before it can execute the method. This ensures that the above sequence of operations cannot occur. Instead, Thread-1 is allowed to complete the method before Thread-2 starts executing it:
1) Thread-1 obtains the monitor lock and increments the counter
2) Thread-2 attempts to obtain the monitor lock but is forced to wait
3) Thread-1 reads counter and returns value, releasing the monitor lock
4) Thread-2 obtains the monitor lock and increments the counter
5) Thread-2 reads counter and returns the value, releasing the monitor lock
In this way, Thread-1 returns a value of 1 and Thread-2 returns a value of 2.

The second step in the above sequence illustrates one of the ways in which a thread can move from the Runnable state to the Not Runnable state. Thread-2 is no longer runnable while it waiting for a lock which is unavailable. Once the lock is released, Thread-2 becomes Runnable again. Another way in which a thread can move between Runnable and Not Runnable states is when a wait-notify pattern is executed. This arises when one thread is producing a resource for which another thread is consumer. The consumer may need to wait until the producer has completed its task. The producer will notify waiting consumers when it has finished. This is best seen through an example. Let us consider a queue which supports two operations
(a) an operation to add random integers to the end of the queue, and
(b) an operation to remove an integer from the head of the queue
We might define a class in the following way:

```
import java.util.*;

public class MyQueue
{
```

```
    private List queue;

    public MyQueue()
    {
        queue = new LinkedList();
    }

    public synchronized void enqueue()
    {
        Integer i = new Integer ((int)Math.floor(100*Math.random()));
        queue.add(i);
        System.out.println ("Added "+i+" to queue");
        notifyAll();
    }

    public synchronized Integer dequeue ()
    {
        Integer val = null;
        while (queue.isEmpty())
        {
            try
            {
                wait();
            }
            catch (InterruptedException ex)
            {
                // ignore
            }
        }
        val = (Integer)queue.remove(0);
        return val;
    }
}
```

The enqueue() method is straightforward. It generates a random integer, adds it to the end of the queue, and notifies waiting threads that it has completed. The dequeue() method is a little more complicated. It first tests the queue to see if it is empty, in which case it waits until a value is added to the queue. Once a value is found, it removes it from the queue and returns it as result. Notice that both methods are synchronized to prevent conflict from concurrent access to the queue.

The key to the correct operation of the queue is the use of wait-notify. These are methods which can be executed only by the thread which holds the monitor lock, so they are often used within synchronized methods. When a thread executes wait(), it releases the monitor lock so that other threads can proceed. The thread has become Not Runnable at this point. When another thread executes notifyAll(), the waiting thread reclaims the monitor lock and becomes Runnable again.

Now let us consider a program which uses different threads to execute the two methods on the queue. We shall first define a class called WriterThread which will be responsible for adding elements to the queue. This class will implement Runnable, and its run() method will add to the queue.

```
public class WriterThread implements Runnable
{

    private MyQueue queue;

    public WriterThread (MyQueue queue)
    {
        this.queue = queue;
    }

    public void run()
    {
        for (int j=0; j < 10; j++)
        {
            queue.enqueue();
        }
    }
}
```

Similarly we can define a class called ReaderThread, whose run() method will take a value from the head of the queue:

```
public class ReaderThread implements Runnable
{
    private MyQueue queue;

    public ReaderThread (MyQueue queue)
    {
        this.queue = queue;
    }

    public void run()
    {
        for (int j=0; j < 10; j++)
        {
            Integer i = queue.dequeue();
            System.out.println ("Took "+i+" from queue");
        }
    }
}
```

Finally, we can define a simple class whose main() method will create and run the two threads.

```
public class Threads
{
    public static void main(String[] args)
    {
        MyQueue q = new MyQueue();
        (new Thread (new WriterThread(q))).start();
        (new Thread (new ReaderThread(q))).start();
    }
}
```

When this program is run, the writer will add ten numbers to the queue, and the reader will take the ten numbers from the queue. In general, though, we cannot predict whether the reader will obtain each value as soon as it is added to the queue, or whether the writer will add two or more items to the queue before the reader takes one. In this example, we do not need to worry too much about such issues. It does point to a more general issue, though, which can have significant consequences. How do we ensure that each thread gets scheduled to run sufficiently often to perform its work ?

A thread may suffer from starvation if other greedy threads claim monitor locks and perform regular long-running operations. Such a situation could be alleviated by the greedy thread giving up control at some point during its processing. The Thread class provides some useful methods for doing that:
- sleep() causes the thread to become Not Runnable for a period of time
- yield() allows the scheduler to run a different thread

Note that the running thread remains Runnable after executing yield(): it simply improves the chances of other threads getting a fair turn. There is a significant difference between sleep() and yield(). If a thread holds a monitor lock, executing yield() will cause it to temporarily give up the lock. This can be very important in cases where you have a long-running synchronized method, for example. On the other hand, a thread continues to hold on to monitor locks when it executes sleep(). Consequently, sleep() is best used when the thread does not hold any monitor locks. Otherwise, it may be impossible for other threads to proceed during the duration of the sleep, and processor utilisation will suffer.

We have seen that use of synchronized methods is important to prevent conflicting access to shared resources. It should also be noted, however, that excessive or incorrect use of synchronization can increase the danger of *deadlock*. Deadlock occurs when two or more Runnable threads are unable to proceed because each is waiting for a monitor lock which is held by one of the others. A simple case is where Thread-1 holds a lock on object-1 and requires the lock on object-2, while Thread-2 holds the lock on object-2 and requires a lock on object-1. Such a case is easily created: let us first define a class called Deadlock1 as follows:

```
public class Deadlock1
{
    public static int d=0;

    public static synchronized void lock1()
    {
        ++d;
    }
}
```

```
    public static synchronized void lock2()
    {
        try
        {
            Thread.sleep(100L);
        }
        catch (InterruptedException ex)
        {
            // ignore
        }
        Deadlock2.lock1();
    }
}
```

We now define a class called Deadlock2 as follows:

```
public class Deadlock2
{
    public static int d=0;

    public static synchronized void lock1()
    {
        ++d;
    }

    public static synchronized void lock2()
    {
        try
        {
            Thread.sleep(100L);
        }
        catch (InterruptedException ex)
        {
            // ignore
        }
        Deadlock1.lock1();
    }
}
```

88

Notice that the method Deadlock1.lock2() requires obtaining the monitor lock on Deadlock1 followed by the monitor lock on Deadlock2, while the method Deadlock2.lock2() requires obtaining the same two monitor locks in the opposite sequence. The use of sleep() introduces a delay between obtaining the two locks, and increases the likelihood of other threads executing conflicting operations in the meantime. Let us now define a class whose run() method obtains the locks in the first sequence:

```
public class Thread1 implements Runnable
{

    public void run()
    {
        while (true)
        {
            Deadlock1.lock2();
            System.out.println ("Incremented Deadlock2.d to " +
                Deadlock2.d);
        }
    }
}
```

Next we define a class whose run() method obtains the same two locks in the opposite order:

```
public class Thread2 implements Runnable
{

    public void run()
    {
        Deadlock2.lock2();
        System.out.println ("Incremented Deadlock1.d to "+Deadlock1.d);
    }
}
```

Finally, we define a class whose main() method will create the two threads:

89

```java
public class Deadlock
{
    public static void main(String[] args)
    {
        (new Thread (new Thread1())).start();
        (new Thread (new Thread2())).start();
    }
}
```

When this program is run, the two threads will very soon become deadlocked. Once deadlock occurs, there is no way of recovering other than by restarting the program. The existence of a deadlock can be confirmed by taking a *thread dump*, which shows the state of each thread, which monitor locks they hold, and which locks they are waiting for. To minimise the risk of deadlock, synchronization should be used only where it is really needed; threads should release monitor locks when they do not need them; and, where it is necessary for threads to hold multiple monitor locks at the same time, they should be made to acquire those locks in a fixed order.

# Chapter 5

# DATABASE FUNDAMENTALS

---

In this chapter we shall look at the fundamental aspects of database architecture, with a particular emphasis on those aspects relating to query processing. In subsequent chapters, we shall discuss in some detail how to express queries and build database applications. But it is important to understand how the database system will process those queries, in order to construct efficient applications.

## 5.1 Database schema

A database is a collection of shared, persistent data. The essential features of a database are:
1) The lifetime of the data generally exceeds the lifetime of the application which creates the data, implying that the data must be stored on disk.
2) The data are shared by many different applications, which may access the database concurrently and may need to access the data in quite different ways. Consequently, the data structures must be designed to support efficient access by all of those applications.
3) It is usually possible for applications to update the database as well as to retrieve data, though the ability to update may be tightly controlled and limited to a few applications. A consequence of allowing updates is that highly complex transaction management mechanisms need to be provided to ensure the integrity of the data and to avoid conflict between applications.

To retrieve data from a database into an application, the data must first be fetched from disk into the database system's memory area, and then transferred to the application. This is an inherently inefficient process, firstly because disk access is slow and secondly because (if the application and the database system reside on different machines) there is a need to transfer data across a network. Database systems provide features to minimise these inefficiencies, but careful design, of both database and applications, is necessary in order to make best use of those features.

Database systems support the concept of a high-level data model, of which the *relational model* is by far the most popular. A data model allows the structure of the data to be described in terms of a *database schema*. Applications express queries in terms of the schema, and the database system will translate those queries into low-level operations against the database (Figure 5.1).

This approach has a number of advantages:
- Application programs can be written quickly using high-level query languages
- Application programmers only need to understand the high-level structure of the data as defined by the schema, they do not need to understand how the data are physically stored on disk
- The database system can provide highly sophisticated query optimisers, which automatically determine the most efficient way to process a query. A good query optimiser can usually find more efficient strategies than a programmer could, because it has access to detailed information about the various data structures provided by the database system.
- The database can be physically reorganised without affecting existing applications. It is only when the schema changes that an application might need to be modified.

Let us now look at the relational data model in some detail.

## 5.2 Relational data model

The relational model, as defined by Edgar Codd in 1970, supports only one conceptual data structure, the *relation*. This data structure is based on the

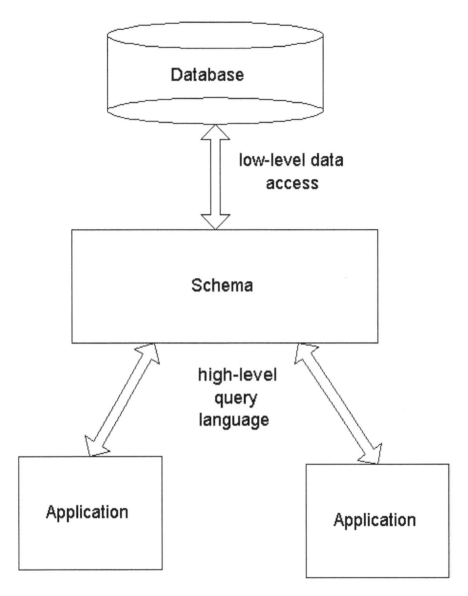

Figure 5.1 Database access via schema

mathematical concept of a relation on two sets, which is defined as a subset of the cartesian product of those sets. In a relational database, each relation is used to represent *entities* of a particular type. For each entity type, the database stores a set of *attributes*. Each attribute has a set of allowed values, known as its *domain*. Technically, a relation is a subset of the cartesian product of the domains of its attributes. In practice, it turns out that each relation can be represented as a table, in which each column represents an attribute. The terms relation and table are often used interchangeably, and we shall refer frequently to tables and columns in later sections of this book. For the present discussion, however, we shall adhere to the more formal terminology of relations and attributes. Similarly, we shall refer to the individual records of a relation as *tuples* rather than rows.

A relational database, then, consists of a set of relations. The schema gives the name of each relation, and the name and domain of each attribute. Generally the domains are limited to simple types such as strings and numbers, meaning that each attribute holds only a single value for each tuple. When this restriction is adhered to, the database is said to be in *first normal form*. First normal form is necessary in order that a relation can be represented as a single table, but it does limit the ability of the data model to express the natural structure of the data. As a result, some relational database systems now support more complex domains such as record and collection types. We shall discuss these further in Chapter 8, but for the moment we shall assume that the database is in first normal form.

An important idea in relational database theory is that of *functional dependency*. We say that an attribute B is functionally dependent on another attribute A (denoted A → B) if any two tuples which have equal values for A must necessarily also have equal values for B. For example, suppose we have a relation called Employee, which has attributes EmployeeID, EmployeeName, DepartmentID, DepartmentName. We can identify the following functional dependencies:

EmployeeID → EmployeeName
EmployeeID → DepartmentID
EmployeeID →DepartmentName
DepartmentID → DepartmentName
DepartmentName → DepartmentID

We are making a few assumptions here. First, that an employee can only belong to one department, which gives rise to the second and third dependencies above. Second, that department names (as well as department identifiers) are unique.

More generally, we can apply the concept of functional dependency to sets of attributes. Thus, a set of attributes T is functionally dependent on a set of attributes S (S → T) if any two rows which have equal values for all attributes in S must also have equal values for all attributes in T. We use the notation RS to denote the set containing all attributes in R and all attributes in S. The process of defining the functional dependencies is made a little easier by using Armstrong's axioms:

- If $X \supseteq Y$, then $X \rightarrow Y$
- If $X \rightarrow Y$, then $XZ \rightarrow YZ$ for any Z
- If $X \rightarrow Y$ and $Y \rightarrow Z$, then $X \rightarrow Z$

In designing a relational database, we first have to decide what information needs to be stored. Having determined that, we need to decide how best to group the various attributes into relations. A common assumption to start from is that all of the relations in a database are derivable from a *universal relation*. Thus, our starting point is a single relation which includes all of the attributes which need to be represented in the database. Functional dependencies then play a central role in deciding how best to decompose that universal relation.

Codd and others have defined various *normal forms*, which specify desirable properties of a database design. Most of these normal forms are defined in terms of functional dependencies. But before we look at normal forms in detail, let us consider an example to illustrate why they are necessary. Taking the example of the Employee relation described above, it might hold the following values:

| EmployeeID | EmployeeName | DepartmentID | DepartmentName |
|------------|--------------|--------------|----------------|
| 0001 | Fred Bloggs | 001 | Sales |
| 0002 | Jane Doe | 001 | Sales |
| 0003 | Fred Bloggs | 002 | Architecture |

The table defines three employees, of whom two happen to have the same name. It also defines two departments, one with two employees and one with a single employee. There are several problems with this design:

96

1) If the name of department 001 changes, say from 'Sales' to 'Sales and Marketing', we need to update two tuples (in general, one tuple for each employee of the department)
2) If we want to add an employee who is not currently assigned to a department, we can only do so by adding null values for departmentID and departmentName. Similarly, to add a new department without adding employees requires specifying null values for employeeID and employeeName.
3) Deleting an employee might have the effect of deleting their department, if the employee is the only one in the department. To delete a department, we have to delete tuples of all the employees in that department, or else assign them to different departments.

Informally, we can see that these complications arise because a single relation is being used to store information about two types of entity (employees and departments). We can avoid update anomalies if we store each entity type in a separate relation. The theory of functional dependencies enables us to be rather more precise about this.

**Keys and superkeys**

A set of attributes S is called a *superkey* of a relation T if S→ X for any set X of attributes from T. In other words, all attributes of a relation are functionally dependent on any superkey. We call S a *candidate key* of T if it is a superkey and if no proper subset of S is a superkey. Thus, a candidate key is a non-redundant superkey. A relation must have at least one candidate key, but it may have several. In any case, one of the candidate keys is chosen to be the *primary key*. An attribute is *prime* if it forms part of at least one candidate key. Otherwise, it is *non-prime*. Keys and superkeys have an important role to play in normalisation theory, which seeks to define desirable properties of a relational schema.

**Representation of relationships**

Databases typically hold data about entities of different kinds, and about the relationships between those entities. For example, employees and departments are related by an employee being a member of a department. We call this relationship a *one-to-many relationship*, because one department may have many employees but a given employee is assigned to only one department at a time. But note that, if we want to maintain historical data, it is likely to be a *many-to-many relationship* because an employee may have been assigned to more than one department over time. The distinction is important because it has a considerable bearing on the way in which relationships are represented in a relational database. If we know that one tuple of relation A can be related to at most one tuple of relation B, we can give A an attribute to hold the primary key value of the related tuple of B. We call this attribute a *foreign key*. This constrains the attribute to hold an existing primary key value from another relation, or else a null value. If, on the other hand, each tuple of either A or B could be related to many tuples of the other relation, we require a different solution. In that case, we can create a new relation C which has separate foreign key attributes linking it to both A and B. In effect, we are breaking down the many-to-many relationship into two one-to-many relationships: one between A and C, and one between B and C.

**Normal forms**

We have already mentioned first normal form, which constrained all attribute values to be atomic-valued. Various higher normal forms are defined to prevent the kind of problems caused by the Employee/Department relation described above. The normal forms impose increasing levels of constraint on the database design, and thus can be seen as enforcing increasingly high-quality designs.

A relation is in *Second Normal Form* if each of its non-prime attributes is fully functionally dependent on each of its candidate keys. We say that A is fully functionally dependent on B if A is functionally dependent on B and A is not functionally dependent on any proper subset of B. For example, suppose a university has a database with information about courses and instructors, and one of the relations is defined as follows:

CourseSection (courseID, courseName, sectionID, instructorID, academicYear, semester)

Let us further suppose that the following functional dependencies apply:

courseID → courseName
courseID, sectionID, academicYear → instructorID, semester

The relation would then have a candidate key of {courseID, sectionID, academicYear}. It is not in Second Normal Form, because the attribute courseName is dependent on courseID alone.

A relation is in *Third Normal Form* if none of its non-prime attributes is transitively dependent on any candidate key. We say that C is transitively dependent on A if, for some set of attributes B, A $\rightarrow$ B and B $\rightarrow$ C. If we consider the Employee/Department relation defined above, we can see that EmployeeID is a candidate key. But EmployeeID $\rightarrow$ DepartmentID $\rightarrow$ DepartmentName, so DepartmentName is transitively dependent on EmployeeID. Consequently, the relation is not in Third Normal Form.

A limitation of Third Normal Form is that it applies only to non-prime attributes. Thus, it still allows for the possibility of transitive dependencies involving prime attributes. For example, suppose we choose to add the date of the final exam as an additional attribute of the CourseSection relation. The following additional functional dependencies apply:

courseID, sectionID, academicYear $\rightarrow$ dateOfExam
dateOfExam $\rightarrow$ academicYear

Hence, the candidate key remains unchanged, and the relation is still in Third Normal Form because there are no transitive dependencies involving non-prime attributes. There is, however, a transitive dependency involving a prime attribute:

courseID, sectionID, academicYear $\rightarrow$ dateOfExam $\rightarrow$ academicYear

This kind of anomaly gives rise to the need for a constraint which is stronger than Third Normal Form. We say that a relation is in *Boyce-Codd Normal Form* if no attribute is functionally dependent on any set of attributes which is not a superkey. For most purposes, Boyce-Codd Normal Form can be regarded as the ideal for a database design, although even more restrictive Fourth and Fifth Normal Forms have been proposed. If a relation is not in Boyce-Codd Normal Form, the same information is liable to be stored in more than place, giving rise to the danger of update anomalies. In practice, database designers will often choose not to adhere to this 'ideal' of design because there are performance advantages in having fewer relations with more attributes. Care must be taken in that case, to ensure that the consistency of the data is maintained when updates occur.

One of the ways of achieving that, as we shall see in Chapter 7, is to allow the database to be updated only through stored procedures.

**Relational languages**

A central feature of the relational model is that it can be viewed as an implementation of first-order logic. If we view the database as a set of predicates, each predicate corresponding to a relation, then we can use the predicate calculus as a language for querying the database. The resulting language is known as the *relational calculus*. Expressions in relational calculus have two parts: tuple variables to describe what should be presented in the result of the query, and a well-formed formula to describe the search condition. For example, suppose we want to find the section numbers and instructors for course CS101 in Spring 2008. We could express the query as follows:

{X.sectionID, X.instructorID | CourseSection(X) ∧ X.courseID = 'CS101' ∧ X.academicYear = '2007-08' ∧ X.semester = 'Spring'}

Now suppose the database has another relation holding details of instructors:

Instructor (instructorID, instructorName, rank, departmentID)

We can now modify the previous query to give the names (rather than identifiers) of the instructors:

{X.sectionID, Y.instructorName | CourseSection(X) ∧ Instructor(Y) ∧ X.courseID = 'CS101' ∧ X.academicYear = '2007-08' ∧ X.semester = 'Spring' ∧ X.instructorID = Y.instructorID}

The relational calculus is important for providing a strong theoretical foundation for the relational model, and has helped in proving the correctness of various algorithms. It also provides a benchmark for all relational database query languages. Codd defines a language to be *relationally complete* if it is at least as expressive as the relational calculus.

The most obvious way to obtain a relationally complete language is to build a language which uses the same constructs as the relational calculus. The best-known example of this approach is QUEL, which was developed for the INGRES database system. QUEL is highly regarded by many database experts, because of its sound theoretical foundation and clear semantics. However, it is not so easy for casual users to learn, and consequently it is not widely used today.

Another approach is to define a set of fundamental high-level operations on relations, which between them are capable of expressing anything which can be done with relational calculus. Indeed, Codd did just that when he proposed the *relational algebra*. The relational algebra consists of the following operations:

- Selection
- Projection
- Cartesian product
- Join
- Division
- Union
- Difference
- Intersection

An important feature of the algebra is that each operation takes one or more relations as operands and returns a relation as result. Consequently, the result of one operation can be used as an operand of a subsequent operation. This allows us to build complex queries as a sequence of relational algebra operations, so that the algebra becomes a powerful query language.

The selection operation selects those tuples of a relation which satisfy a specified condition. It is written
$\sigma_{condition}(\text{relation})$
For example, suppose we want to select from CourseSection just the sections of course CS101. We can express this as follows:
$\sigma_{courseID='CS101'}(\text{CourseSection})$

The projection operation selects all the tuples of a relation, but returns only the listed attributes in the result. It is written
$\pi_{attributeList}(\text{relation})$
Very often, it is combined with a selection operation, as in the following example which returns the instructors who have taught CS101:
$\pi_{instructorID}(\sigma_{courseID='CS101'}(\text{CourseSection}))$

The cartesian product operates on two operand relations, and returns a result containing all the attributes from each of the operands, and all tuples which can be formed by concatenating a tuple of the first operand with a tuple of the second operand. It is written

Relation1 × Relation2

In practice, the cartesian product is rarely used on its own because we seldom want to concatenate *all* pairs of tuples from the two operands. More commonly, we want to concatenate just those pairs which satisfy a condition. An operation which does that is called a *join*. There are various kinds of join operation, of which the most commonly used is the *equi-join*. An equi-join is a join whose condition uses only equality comparisons between attributes. It is written

Relation1 $\bowtie_{condition}$ Relation2

For example, to find the names of instructors who have taught CS101:

$\pi_{Instructor.instructorID}(\sigma_{courseID='CS101'}(CourseSection) \bowtie_{CourseSection.InstructorID = Instructor.instructorID} Instructor)$

The division operation is another which operates on two operand relations. The first operand should contain all the attributes of the second, and at least one additional attribute. The resulting relation contains just those attributes of the first operand which are not present in the second, and contains the tuples of the first operand which match all tuples of the second. It is written

Relation1 ÷ Relation2

For example, suppose we want find the courses which have been taught by all professors in department D101. We can express the query as follows:

$\pi_{courseID, instructorID}(CourseSection) \div \pi_{instructorID}(\sigma_{rank='Professor' \wedge departmentID='D101'}(Instructor))$

The operators of union, difference and intersection are the usual operators of set theory, operating on a relation as a set of tuples. A requirement of all of these operators is that the operands be *union-compatible*. That is, they must have the same number of attributes, and each attribute of the first operand must have the same domain as the corresponding attribute of the second operand. Union (A $\cup$ B) returns all those tuples which are present in one or both of the operands; difference (A − B) returns those which are present in A and not in B; and intersection (A $\cap$ B) returns just those tuples which are present in both operands.

The relational algebra has been shown to be relationally complete. In fact, this requires only five operators ($\sigma$, $\pi$, $\times$, $\cup$, -): join is logically equivalent to cartesian product followed by selection; intersection can be defined in terms of difference ($A \cap B \equiv A - (A - B)$); and, less obviously, division can be defined in terms of cartesian product, difference and projection:

$$\pi_{\text{courseID, instructorID}}(\text{CourseSection}) \div \pi_{\text{instructorID}}(\sigma_{\text{rank='Professor'} \wedge}$$
$$_{\text{departmentID='D101'}}(\text{Instructor})) \equiv$$
$$\pi_{\text{courseID}}(\text{CourseSection}) - \pi_{\text{courseID}}((\pi_{\text{instructorID}}(\sigma_{\text{rank='Professor'} \wedge}$$
$$_{\text{departmentID='D101'}}(\text{Instructor})) \times \pi_{\text{courseID}}(\text{CourseSection})) -$$
$$\pi_{\text{courseID, instructorID}}(\text{CourseSection}))$$

Nevertheless, these other operations (especially join) are used so frequently that it is important for a database system to be able to implement them directly.

The relational algebra is important because it gives us a means of implementing a language which is as expressive as relational calculus. Indeed, it could also be used directly as a query language itself, and some experimental systems did use it in that way. However, experience has shown that relational algebra is not particularly easy for beginners to learn. Moreover, commercial systems generally require a number of additional operations to be added to the language, which would make the algebra quite cumbersome. So, in practice, its role is to provide a set of efficient operations which together are capable of implementing a more user-friendly query language. In Section 5.4, we shall look at the implementation of relational algebra operations. But first, let us take a higher-level view of how an application program interacts with the database.

## 5.3 Query processing

Figure 5.2 illustrates the main components of a typical database application. The diagram is deliberately simplified, with the aim of illustrating general concepts rather than considering all the details of a particular environment.

The application runs as a user process which requires access to a database. The database generally runs on dedicated hardware, so (except for toy databases) there will almost certainly be a network connection between the application and the database. The application logs in to the database, at which point a server process is created with the purpose of handling database requests for that user. Two potential performance bottlenecks should be immediately apparent. First, the server process is going to have to fetch data from the database which is on disk. Second, the user process and server process need to send data across a network, which is slow primarily due to network latency but also due to the need to perform conversions between database data types and application program data types. In order that the database system performs efficiently, two key principles can be identified:

- Disk accesses should be kept to a minimum
- Interactions between the user process and the server process should be coarse-grained, i.e., there should be one request for a lot of processing rather than many requests each for a little processing.

One way of minimising disk accesses is to implement efficient algorithms to locate on disk just the data which are required for processing the query. Rather than fetching a lot of data from disk and searching in memory, we want to fetch only the necessary data. To aid this process, a database provides index structures, which can be likened to the index of a book, to quickly locate the required information. Although there is some overhead in searching an index, it is usually much faster to find the required information via a suitably structured index than by random searching. We shall describe some common algorithms a little later, but there is another important technique for reducing disk access. If we have fetched data to process a prior query, there is no need to fetch the same data again to process the next query. Instead, we can cache the data in memory, so that it can be more quickly retrieved. Modern database systems have very sophisticated mechanisms for caching data. Retrieving data from memory is so much faster than fetching from disk that it is crucial to make good use of cache memory.

When an application is connected to a database over a network, each call to the database suffers a performance hit due to network delays. Consequently it is important to keep the number of calls to a minimum. For example, suppose we need to run a database query which returns 1000 rows as its result. A highly inefficient implementation might work as follows:

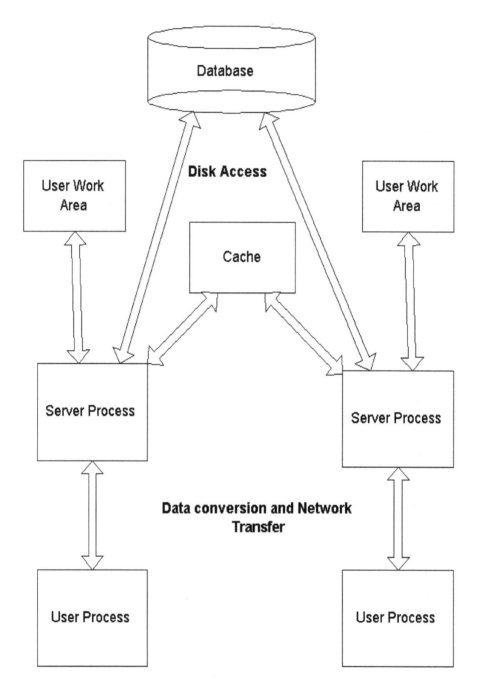

Figure 5.2 Database application architecture

Call to the server process to execute the query
Repeat
    Call to server process to fetch next row of result
    Process row in application
Until no more rows to fetch

With 1000 rows in the result, we are making at least 1001 calls across the network (in fact, there will be more due to the need to set up the query and close it down again). We can reduce this number considerably by implementing buffering. Thus, rather than fetch only one row at a time, we can fetch several at once, in anticipation that the application will need to process subsequent rows.

As a further example, the application may frequently need to execute a logical unit of work in which, say, it runs a query and then updates two different tables. This could be implemented by first calling the server to execute the query, then fetching the result rows from the server, then calling the server again to update the first table, and finally making yet another call to update the second table. It would be far more efficient if we could store the whole unit of work on the server as a *stored procedure*. The application can then make a single call to the server to execute the stored procedure.

We shall discuss stored procedures in detail in Chapter 7. In Chapter 9, we shall look in detail at ways of querying a database from Java, and how these optimisations can be applied in a Java application. But next let us examine how some of the most frequently-used operations of relational algebra can be efficiently implemented.


## 5.4 Implementation of relational algebra operations

The three most frequently-used operations of relational algebra are selection, projection and join. Of these, projection is relatively trivial to implement, but selection and join have been the subject of a great deal of work on query optimisation. Those two operations are important, both because of the frequency with which they are used and because of the vast difference in performance between the most efficient and least efficient implementations.

There are two common algorithms for implementing the selection operation. The first (rather simple-minded) approach involves a full table scan, i.e., the entire table is fetched from the database, and the selection condition is applied to each row in order to determine which of them qualify for inclusion in the result. If the table has, say, ten rows, this algorithm is going to be perfectly adequate. Indeed, it may even be the most efficient way to execute the query. If, on the other hand, the table has a million rows, then it will be unacceptably slow for most applications.

The alternative algorithm for selection is to make use of an index. For example, suppose we want to list the sections of course CS101 from the CourseSection table. If we construct an index which tells us the physical location on disk of each row of CourseSection which has a given value of courseID, we can then simply search the index and then directly locate the required rows. This can be much faster than doing a full table scan. Specifically, it will be faster if
1) Searching the index is much faster than searching the table, and
2) As a result of searching the index first, we only need to fetch a small proportion of the rows of the table
We shall describe the structure and use of an index more fully in the next section. For now, we shall simply state that the time taken to search an index is almost independent of the size of the table being indexed. Thus, the larger the table the greater the potential benefit of the index. Nevertheless, it is important to bear in mind the second point listed above: if the selection condition is one which is satisfied by 90% of the rows in the table, we are going to end up fetching nearly all of the rows anyway.

There are three main algorithms for implementing the equi-join operator, and some of them can also be adapted for implementing other types of join. The first algorithm is called the nested-loop join algorithm. It works as follows (for joining tables A and B on a common column c):

result := empty set
for each row $r_a$ of table A
    for each row $r_b$ of table B
        if $r_a.c = r_b.c$ then
            concatenate $r_a$ and $r_b$ and add to result

This algorithm can be quite effective if table B is sufficiently small to be held in memory. In that case, we only need to fetch B once. As the rows of

A are fetched from disk, each can be compared with the rows of B and then discarded (once any matches have been added to the result). We end up having to fetch each row of each table only once, which may be acceptable. Performance will be very poor, however, when B is very large. In that case we would have to fetch B a bit at a time, throwing away one set of rows in order to fetch the next set. That would mean fetching each row of B many times in order to compare with each row of A.

When B is large, the nested loop join is much more efficient when we can make use of an index on B. Then, for each row of A, we simply look up the index to find the matching rows of B. Each row of B is then fetched only when it matches a row of A. If there are many matches it may still be inefficient but, as long as there are relatively few matching pairs, it performs well.

The second join algorithm is called sort-merge. This algorithm works by sorting each of the operands and then finding the matching pairs by means of a merge operation. The algorithm is defined as follows:

```
sort A in ascending order of c
sort B in ascending order of c
set r_a = first row of A
set r_b = first row of B
while (r_a != null and r_b != null) do
    if r_a.c = r_b.c then
        concatenate r_a and r_b and add to result
    if r_a.c <= r_b.c then
        set r_a = next row of A (null if A has no more rows)
    else
        set r_b = next row of B (null if B has no more rows)
end while
```

Sort-merge is reasonably efficient, especially if the tables can be fetched in order of the join attribute (thus eliminating the need to sort). Once the tables are sorted, each row is accessed only once in computing the join.

The third join algorithm is called hash join. A hash function is applied to the join attribute, and the rows are partitioned into buckets according to the value of the hash function. We then only need to look for matches among rows which are in the same bucket. The algorithm works as follows:

```
for each row r of A
    place r in bucket h(r.c)
for each row r_b of B
    for each row r_a of A in bucket h(r_b.c)
        if r_a.c = r_b.c then
            concatenate r_a and r_b and add to result
```

Compared with the nested loop algorithm, hash join has the advantage that we only need to compare those rows which have the same hash value. Nevertheless, both algorithms depend on being able to hold the inner table in memory - otherwise, it may be necessary to fetch the same data repeatedly. We can make the choice to store only pointers to the rows in the hash buckets: that reduces the memory requirement but necessitates additional disk accesses to fetch the rows when a match is found.

### 5.5 Index structures

An index is stored using one of the variants of the B-tree structure. A B-tree is a structure which is designed to remain balanced, regardless of the pattern of update operations applied to the data. Tree structures in general are well-known to be efficient for searching as long as they are balanced, but can perform poorly if one part of the tree is much deeper than another.

Figure 5.3 illustrates the structure of a $B^+$-tree index, which is a structure particularly well suited to supporting a database index. In this example, let us suppose that the database contains a table of Person records, and that there is a requirement to provide fast access to individual records by last name. The tree is designed so that a particular name can be located quickly, by searching from the root. Each non-root node consists of alternating pointers and search keys, with the pointers pointing to a node at the level below. The leaf nodes have a similar structure, but in their case the pointers point to the database records which have the specified key. Since the pointers outnumber the keys by one in each leaf node, the final pointer can be used to link the leaf nodes together. This means that the same structure can be used to efficiently read the entire table in order of last name.

Let us suppose that we need to fetch the record of the person named 'Lee'. We start by fetching the root node. The structure of the tree is such that

Harper and all preceding names are found by following the left branch, while all subsequent names are found by following the right branch. This brings us to the node with search keys 'Johns' and 'Moore'. This node enables us to select from three leaf nodes: since Lee is between Johns and Moore in alphabetical order, we navigate to the middle one of the three. From this leaf node, we find the key we are looking for and follow the corresponding pointer to the record in the database.

Accessing records via an index is often faster than accessing the table directly, because it enables us to find a particular record using fewer disk accesses. The nodes of a B-tree are typically much larger in practice than those shown in the illustrative example above. In practice, each node must fit within one disk block, but we want to store as many keys as possible into a single node. In this way, the tree will have few levels, even when there are many leaf nodes; and to access a record in
the database, we require one disk access for each level in the tree, plus a further disk access for the record itself. If the table is very large, the saving can be considerable.

A $B^+$-tree of order p is defined to be one in which a maximum of p pointers (hence p-1 key values) can be held in each node. It must also have the following properties:
- Each non-leaf node (other than the root) must have at least $\lceil p/2 \rceil$ pointers
- The root must have at least 2 pointers
- Each leaf node must have at least $\lfloor p/2 \rfloor$ key values

Thus, non-root nodes are only required to be half-full, and the root node can be considerably less full than that. It might be thought that the number of levels of a $B^+$-tree would be greatly affected by the fullness or otherwise of the nodes, but in fact that is not always the case. We shall illustrate this by an example. Suppose our block size is 1024 bytes, and we wish to build an index for a table of 10,000 records, where 6 bytes are required for each pointer and 20 bytes for each key value. This means that a full node will contain 40 pointers and 39 keys. From the definition of a $B^+$-tree given above, let us now determine the minimum and maximum number of levels for the index. We claim that, for this example, the $B^+$-tree will always have a root node, a leaf level and exactly one intermediate level. This can be quickly demonstrated by *reductio ad absurdum*.

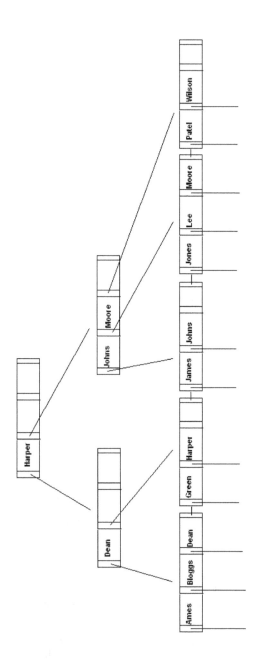

Figure 5.3 Example of a B$^+$-tree index

Suppose, first of all, that the tree has no intermediate level. Then at most, the root can have 40 pointers to leaf nodes, and each leaf can have 39 pointers to database records. Thus there can be a maximum of 1560 records in the database table, which contradicts our statement that there are 10,000 records.

Now let us suppose that the tree has two intermediate levels. The root must have at least 2 pointers to nodes at the level below. Each of those 2 nodes must have at least 20 pointers to nodes at the second intermediate level, giving at least 40 nodes at that level. And if each of the 40 nodes has a minimum of 20 pointers to leaf nodes, we must have at least 800 leaf nodes in all. Now since each leaf node has at least 20 pointers to database records, the database table must have at least 16,000 records. Again, this contradicts our assumption that there are 10,000 records in the table.

We have thus proved that, for this particular example, the $B^+$-tree index must have exactly two levels, in addition to the root. This suggests that we really do not need to worry much about whether or not the nodes are full to capacity, because it has little bearing on the performance of the index. More important is an efficient algorithm for updating the index in line with updates to the underlying table. Whenever a record is inserted into, or deleted from, the table, a corresponding update must be made to the index. Here we shall outline an algorithm for handling an insertion. When a record is inserted into the table, it is always necessary to insert a key/pointer pair at the leaf level. As long as there is space available in the appropriate leaf node, this is all that needs to be done – the upper levels of the tree are unaffected. The complication arises when the leaf node is already full to capacity, i.e., it already has p-1 key values and p pointers. The simple solution is to split the leaf node into two, creating one leaf node with $\lceil p/2 \rceil$ key values and one with $\lfloor p/2 \rfloor$ key values. This preserves the $B^+$-tree property, by maintaining the required minimum capacity. But because there is now an extra leaf node, it does mean that we need also an extra key and pointer at the level above. We can handle the insertion of key and pointer into the upper-level node in the same way as for the leaf node. If the node is already full, it is split and a new key is inserted into the level above. This process continues until either there is room to insert a new key without splitting, or we split the root node and create an extra level to contain the new root. If we split the root, the new root will contain only two pointers – but this still adheres to the $B^+$-tree property.

The algorithm described is very simple to implement, and it does maintain the properties of the B⁺-tree. Nevertheless, it has the weakness that a new level may be created before it is strictly necessary to do so. Consequently, more complex algorithms are generally used in practice. As an alternative to node splitting, a rotation algorithm can be applied, whereby keys are redistributed from full nodes to neighbouring nodes which are less full. When this is done, the search keys in the level above must be adjusted so that the navigation to leaf nodes still operates correctly.

## 5.6 Steps in query processing

Let us now look in more detail at how the server process goes about processing a query (see Figure 5.2). The following steps are required:
- Parse the query, to identify the operations to be carried out
- Develop a query plan, choosing the best order of operations and the best algorithm for each operation
- Execute the query plan

In the previous two sections, we have discussed the main algorithms and the importance of index structures for implementing certain algorithms. Up to now, we have not paid much attention to the importance of the cache. In fact, the cache plays a vital role in all stages of query processing by keeping track of the following kinds of information:
- Data definitions and file information
- Query statements and execution plans
- Recently accessed data blocks

Along with data definitions, the cache will keep details of the size of each relation and the number of distinct values of certain attributes. This information is vital for determining the sizes of operand and result relations for each operation, and thus for choosing the most efficient query plan. For example, an index is likely to be very useful when selecting one record from 100,000; but not when selecting 50 records from 100.

Certain queries tend to be executed repeatedly. Rather than recomputing a query plan each time a query is submitted, the query optimiser can cache query plans so that they are available for use the next time. It may also keep statistics on how well the chosen plan performed in practice – if the plan was much worse than it predicted, it may discard that plan and compute another one based on revised information.

113

If you execute the same query 10 times, you will find that it takes longer to run the first time. A marked improvement in response time can usually be observed when the query is submitted a second time, but thereafter it will run at approximately the same speed each time. The reason for this is that data blocks are cached when they are fetched from the database. So if the next query needs to access the same data blocks, it can find them in the cache rather than having to access disk. In practical applications, it is rare for a user to execute the same query ten times in succession. But different users may need to run the same query, and a given user will often need to run a sequence of related queries which access some of the same data blocks. In addition, there are certain blocks which are accessed very frequently and are likely to be in the cache at all times – the root node of an index is an obvious example.

## 5.7 Transaction management

So far we have focused on operations which retrieve data from the database. A database system also needs to handle operations which update the data, which adds an additional layer of complexity. Managing updates is difficult because it introduces the possibility of conflict between different users who are accessing the same data. There are also issues around allowing users to change their mind about an update, and making sure that an update is handled correctly even when the system crashes in the middle of carrying it out. The concept of a *transaction* helps to solve these difficulties.

A transaction is a logical unit of work which may update the state of the database. Any database update takes place within the context of a transaction. Transactions should obey the so-called ACID properties:
1) Atomicity: the update operations in a given transaction are all applied at once; either all of them go ahead or none of them do.
2) Consistency: when the database is updated, it should be left in a consistent state, not violating any of the integrity constraints defined in the database.
3) Isolation: a transaction should not see the changes made by other transactions which are still executing; this property is the vaguest, and can be implemented to varying degrees in practice.

4) Durability: once a transaction has been committed, its changes will not be lost, even in the event of a system failure.

The structure of a transaction is as follows:

```
begin transaction
  operation
  operation
  ......
  operation
commit or rollback
```

When a transaction is committed, all of its update operations are carried out and become visible to other users. If the transaction is instead rolled back, the updates are thrown away and never written to the database. The decision to commit or rollback effectively ends one transaction and begins another. Thus, the 'begin transaction' is often implicit.

When multiple users are accessing the database concurrently, the system must interleave the operations of the various transactions in order to provide satisfactory response times to all users. This sequence of operations executed by the system is called a *schedule*. This raises the question of what makes a schedule correct or incorrect.

We say that two schedules are equivalent if one can be derived from the other by exchanging pairs of adjacent, non-conflicting operations. Operations are non-conflicting if either of the following conditions apply:
- They access different data
- Both are read operations

A schedule in which the transactions are executed one at a time, with no interleaving of operations, is known as a *serial schedule*. Any schedule which is equivalent to a serial schedule is called *serialisable*. When a database system enforces full isolation between transactions, it guarantees serialisability of its schedules. Serialisability can be guaranteed by implementing the *two-phase locking* protocol. Transactions acquire locks on all data they access – shared locks for read-only access, and exclusive locks for write access. Under two-phase locking, all locks are acquired during the first phase, and none are released until the second phase. Although it guarantees correctness, two-phase locking can limit the throughput of transactions because time is spent waiting for locks to become available. It is also possible for deadlock to occur. Performance will tend to be particularly poor if there are long-running transactions. Consequently it can sometimes be beneficial to trade a degree of correctness for improved performance. Let us now look at the consequences of relaxing the serialisability requirement.

The first step in relaxing serialisability is to allow so-called *phantom reads*. These occur when a transaction executes the same read operation twice, and the second time it returns additional data. In between the two read operations, another transaction has inserted data and committed its changes. Consider the following schedule:

Transaction 1 reads all employees in the 'Sales' department
Transaction 2 inserts a new employee who belongs to the 'Sales' department
Transaction 2 commits
Transaction 1 reads all employees in the 'Sales' department

The schedule is not serialisable: transaction 2 has been allowed to go ahead without waiting for transaction 1 to complete, but the consequence is that transaction 1 sees slightly inconsistent results. Depending on requirements, this trade-off may or may not be considered worthwhile.

We can go a little further and allow *non-repeatable reads*. This means that, if transaction 1 executes the same read operation twice (as in the previous example), it can not only see additional data but can even see changes in the data already read. If this is allowed, performance is further improved but the impact on correctness is greater.

A further relaxation allows *dirty reads*. A dirty read occurs when a transaction reads changes that have been made by another transaction which has not yet committed. This represents a much more serious level of incorrectness, because the updating transaction may eventually be rolled back. Thus, the reading transaction would obtain data that never properly existed in the database. Some database systems, such as Oracle, do not support an isolation level which would allow the possibility of dirty reads.

Approaches based on acquiring locks before data access are known as *pessimistic* concurrency control algorithms. They work well for short transactions, especially when there are many conflicts, but are not very suitable for environments in which users are browsing through a graphical user interface. In such environments, users may leave the application at a time when they hold locks, and possibly not return for several minutes or even longer. In these circumstances, a more appropriate solution is *optimistic* concurrency control. This assumes that conflicts are rare, and that the overhead of locking is unnecessary. Instead, read-only transactions go ahead without locking, and conflicts involving updating transactions are checked when the transaction commits. There is a risk (usually small) that a transaction will fail to commit, but this is outweighed by the improved performance seen by the majority of transactions.

## 5.8 Database schema example

We shall conclude this chapter by defining a database schema for a road distribution company. This schema will provide the basis for illustrating database queries in Chapters 6 and 7. We shall assume that the company operates a number of locations, each of which may be a factory, warehouse or retail store. Between any two locations the company operates one or more routes. Each route has a known length (in both distance and time), height limit and weight limit: thus it is assumed that the shortest route will normally be chosen, but larger vehicles may be forced to take a longer route. A route is composed of a number of legs, each leg taking a specified road in a particular direction. The company owns a number of vans of various types, and employs drivers to drive those vans. The database is to keep track of blocks of time on each day where a van is available for use, having not yet been assigned to a journey. Similarly, it will keep track of blocks of time when a driver is due to work but has not yet been assigned to a journey. One of the important requirements for the database system is, for each required journey, to find a driver who is available to undertake the journey and a van which is available for the same period.

By convention, we shall describe the database schema by giving the table names in upper case, followed by a list of their columns in parentheses. Those columns which form part of the primary key are underlined. Columns which are foreign keys are, by convention, given names beginning with 'fk_'. The schema is as follows:

LOCATION (loc_id, loc_name, loc_type, easting, northing, photograph)
ROUTE (route_id, fk_start_loc, fk_end_loc, distance, journey_time, weight_limit, height_limit, route_map)
ROUTE_LEG (fk_route_id, leg_num, road_name, direction, length)

VAN (licence_num, fk_van_type, fk_base_loc)
VAN_TYPE (van_type_id, make, model, description, weight, height)
DRIVER (driver_id, name, fk_base_loc)
TIMESLOT (hour)
WORKING_HOURS (fk_driver_id, day, fk_start_hour, fk_end_hour,
fk_route_id)
VAN_HOURS (fk_licence_num, day, fk_start_hour, fk_end_hour,
fk_route_id)
BOOKING (fk_driver_id, day, fk_start_hour, fk_licence_num, fk_route_id,
fk_end_hour, booked_by, comments)

The position of each location is defined by its easting and northing. A photograph is also stored so that it can be more easily recognised. Since the definition of a route is in general quite complex (it comprises many legs), a map is provided to give a clearer description of each route. Both drivers and vans are given base locations, so that they can be assigned routes which start at their bases. The timeslot table is an example of a *static table*. It is pre-loaded with a fixed set of values and should not normally be updated. Its purpose is to support data validation in other tables, via foreign key constraints. The working hours table, for example, defines blocks of time in terms of a start hour and end hour. These hours (and similarly those in the van hours table) are foreign keys to the timeslot table. Note that both van hours and working hours have a column which is a foreign key to the route table. Initially, both vans and drivers are free, so fk_route_id will be set to null. When they are assigned to a journey for a block of time, fk_route_id will be assigned a non-null value. At that point, an entry will also be added to the booking table.

You may have noticed that much of the information in the booking table is also held in the working hours and van hours tables. However, the booking table allows for additional details to be recorded about the booking. In addition, it makes querying easier for two reasons:
a)  Information on the van and the driver are both available in the booking table, whereas van_hours and working_hours would need to be joined.
b)  The route is always non-null in the booking table, which means that it can be queried without worrying about additional checks for null values.
In Chapter 6, we shall see how a variety of powerful queries can be easily expressed against this schema. On the other hand, considerable care must be taken when updating the database, in particular to ensure that the

booking table remains consistent with van_hours and working_hours. We shall explore this issue in detail in Chapter 7.

# Chapter 6

# SQL

_____

In the previous chapter we described the relational algebra, which provides a set of operations for querying a relational database. The operations of the relational algebra have a well-defined semantics, and increasingly efficient implementations have been developed over the years. Relational algebra could also be used as a query language, and it was used as such in some early experimental systems, but it is quite difficult for general users to master. What is needed instead is a more declarative language which is easier to use and can be mapped into relational algebra by the query language compiler or interpreter. Among the various languages that have been proposed, SQL is the one that has by now been universally accepted as the de facto standard.

SQL was originally developed at IBM Research Laboratories, as the query language for System R. System R was one of the earliest implementations of the relational data model, and its influence can still be seen in the leading products of today, such as Oracle. In those days, the language was known as SEQUEL (Structured English QUEry Language). Though the name was subsequently shortened to SQL (Structured Query Language), the original pronunciation has been retained. SQL has been criticised by some purists, including Codd himself, for its imperfect implementation of the relational model, but experience has shown it to be relatively easy to learn and very effective both for ad hoc querying of a database and for building sophisticated applications.

Although SQL is often described as a query language, it is actually capable of far more than just querying the database. It can be used to define and

120

modify the structure of the tables; to insert, delete or modify data in the tables; and to carry out a variety of database administration tasks - in addition to searching and retrieving from the database tables. In developing Java applications, we are primarily interested in processing queries and updates on the database tables, but it is also necessary to create and maintain the tables. Sometimes a Java application will also need to create temporary tables in the course of processing. We therefore begin by briefly outlining the SQL statements for creating, altering and dropping tables (this aspect of SQL is called the data definition language, or DDL). We shall then look in greater detail at the statements for querying and updating the tables (the data manipulation language, or DML).

## 6.1 Data definition in SQL

SQL provides statements which allow us to define tables; alter the structure of tables; drop existing tables from the database; and perform other data definition functions. Let us first look at how we can create new tables in the database, which is done by means of the CREATE TABLE statement.

The basic form of the CREATE TABLE statement is

CREATE TABLE table_name (column_name domain constraint, column_name domain constraint, ......)

Some database vendors support extensions to this syntax to specify how and where the table should be stored, but that is beyond the scope of this book. The table name and column names are all identifiers, for which the usual kind of naming conventions apply. The precise details vary from one vendor to another, but it is usually valid to use a name made up of a letter followed by a sequence of letters, digits and underscore characters. There is sometimes a limit on the length of an identifier. The constraint clause is used to specify additional constraints on the values which can be stored in a column. Supported constraint types typically include the following:

- *null value constraint* ("NULL" or "NOT NULL") indicates whether or not null values are permitted in the column.
- *unique constraint* specifies that all values in the column must be distinct

- *primary key constraint* specifies that values must be unique and not null. In addition, only one primary key is allowed per table. The primary key can be used to create references to the table through foreign keys in another table
- *foreign key constraint* specifies that the values stored in a column must be either null or existing values in the primary key column of another table
- *check constraint* specifies that any value must be in a certain range (for numeric or date types) or must be one of an enumerated list of values (for string types)

The domain determines the values which can be stored in the column, in terms of both type and size. For example, "strings of length no more than 20", "integers of up to 6 digits". Again, the precise data types vary from one vendor to another, but the following are typical:

VARCHAR(n) – allows strings of length up to n, where n is an integer
NUMBER(n) – allows integers of up to n digits
NUMBER(n,m) – a fixed-point number with n digits, of which m are after the decimal point
DATE – allows dates, sometimes with a time component included
CLOB – allows very long strings, such as documents
BLOB – allows large binary objects such as images

Some vendors are now supporting collection types. The handling of these, and of CLOB and BLOB types, varies considerably from one vendor to another. Consequently, we shall focus in this chapter on string, numeric and date types. Collections and large objects will be discussed later, focusing on the approach taken in Oracle.

Deleting a table is done using the DROP TABLE statement as follows:

DROP TABLE table_name

A complication with dropping a table is that there may be existing constraints defined on other tables, which refer to the table which is being dropped. In that case, it is possible to specify that any such constraints should be dropped before dropping the table, thus:

DROP TABLE table_name CASCADE CONSTRAINTS

Sometimes we need to alter the definition of an existing table, which may or may not contain data. Such changes include adding columns; dropping columns; changing the definition of columns; renaming columns; and changing the constraints on the table. All of these changes can be handled using different variations of the ALTER TABLE statement. To add columns to a table, we use the following:

ALTER TABLE table_name ADD (column_name domain, column_name domain,…)

To drop a column, we use the following:

ALTER TABLE table_name DROP COLUMN column_name

To change the definition of columns,

ALTER TABLE table_name MODIFY (column_name new_domain, column_name new_domain, …..)

To rename a column,

ALTER TABLE table_name RENAME old_column_name TO new_column_name

To add a primary key constraint to a table,

ALTER TABLE table_name ADD (PRIMARY KEY (column_name, column_name, ….))

To add a foreign key constraint to a table,

ALTER TABLE table_name ADD (FOREIGN KEY (column_name, column_name, ….) REFERENCES table_name)

It is generally much easier to change the structure of an empty table than it is to change the structure of a table which contains data. That is because the existing data in the table may conflict with the new definition of the table. The following issues need to be considered:

123

- we can always drop columns, but doing so may cause dependent constraints to be lost.
- we can add new columns but, if the table contains data and the new columns will be assigned null values, the new columns must not be constrained to disallow null values.
- we can change the domain of a column as long as the new domain includes all existing values: thus, for example, a string-valued column can have its size increased but not decreased.
- we can add a primary key to a table, as long as the table does not already have a primary key and the proposed key does not include any null or duplicate values.
- we can add a foreign key to a table if the proposed foreign key contains only null values or existing values of the referenced primary key.

Sometimes none of the properties of an entity is suitable for use as a primary key. In such cases, we may introduce an extra column, which has no semantic meaning but acts solely as an identifier or primary key. A simple and effective way of supporting these identifiers is to use a sequence. A sequence is a counter, which generates unique integer values. Typically, it initialises the counter to one, and increments it each time a new integer is requested. The syntax for creating a sequence is:

CREATE SEQUENCE sequence_name

Equivalently,

CREATE SEQUENCE sequence_name START WITH 1 INCREMENT BY 1

Different values can be specified for the starting value and increment step if required.

## 6.2 Query statements in SQL

We shall illustrate the various features of SQL by means of example queries, written against the database introduced in the previous chapter. We repeat the list of tables below for convenience:

124

LOCATION (loc_id, loc_name, loc_type, easting, northing, photograph)
ROUTE (route_id, fk_start_loc, fk_end_loc, distance, journey_time, weight_limit, height_limit, route_map)
ROUTE_LEG (fk_route_id, leg_num, road_name, direction, length)
VAN (licence_num, fk_van_type, fk_base_loc)
VAN_TYPE (van_type_id, make, model, description, weight, height)
DRIVER (driver_id, name, fk_base_loc)
TIMESLOT (hour)
WORKING_HOURS (fk_driver_id, day, fk_start_hour, fk_end_hour, fk_route_id)
VAN_HOURS (fk_licence_num, day, fk_start_hour, fk_end_hour, fk_route_id)
BOOKING (fk_driver_id, day, fk_start_hour, fk_licence_num, fk_route_id, fk_end_hour, booked_by, comments)


**6.2.1 Simple queries against a single table**

The simplest SQL queries take the form

SELECT [DISTINCT] column_list
FROM table
WHERE condition

The meaning of such a query is to retrieve from the specified table those rows which match the stated condition, and include in the result only those columns which are listed in the SELECT clause. The keyword DISTINCT is optional. If present, it indicates that any duplicate rows are to be removed from the result. Note that, even though the original table has all distinct rows, the result of a query may contain duplicates when the SELECT clause does not include all of the columns. The following is an example of a query against a single table:

**Query 1**
SELECT loc_name, easting, northing
FROM location
WHERE loc_type = 'Distribution Centre'

A convenient shorthand, when all columns are required in the result, is to use the syntax "SELECT *". Thus,

**Query 2**
SELECT *
FROM location
WHERE loc_type = 'Distribution Centre'

Sometimes we need a way to compare the value of a column with a literal string which contains a single quote character. The problem with this is that, if we simply enclose the string in single quotes, the quote within the string will be interpreted as ending the string. To indicate to the compiler or interpreter that a quote is to be included in the string, we need to write two consecutive single quotes, as in the following example:

**Query 3**
SELECT *
FROM location
WHERE loc_name = 'Bishop''s Stortford'

The condition in the WHERE clause is made up of simple conditions connected by AND and OR. The simple conditions involve comparisons between two expressions (usually a column and a constant), with the comparison operator being one of <, <=, =, >= and >. When comparing string values, it is also possible to select values which match a given regular expression. This is done by using the LIKE operator. The operand on the right-hand side of LIKE is a string which can include wildcard symbols ' _ ' (which matches a single character) and '%' (which matches any sequence of characters). For example,

**Query 4**
SELECT *
FROM driver
WHERE name like '%Bloggs%'

Since the characters '%'and ' _ ' have special meanings as wildcards, an additional construct is needed when we want to include those characters in a literal string. We can add an 'escape' clause to the query, to indicate that a particular character is to be interpreted as the escape character: then by including that character immediately before '%' or ' _ ', we are indicating that a wildcard is not intended. For example, suppose we wish to find the van type whose description includes the string '100%'.

**Query 5**
SELECT *
FROM van_type
WHERE description like '%100\%%' escape '\'

Since the backslash has been declared as the escape character, the sequence
'\%' can be used to indicate an instance of the percent symbol with the
literal string. The other two occurences of '%' are wildcards, as usual. Thus,
the query will find all van types whose description consists of any string
followed by '100%' followed by any string.

There is a further complication where null values might be present, because
the relational data model implements a three-valued logic (true/false/null).
A comparison between two non-null values will always return a result of
either true or false, but a comparison with null returns a result of null. The
value null can be thought of as 'Unknown' (or 'Undefined'), so it is logical
that a comparison with an unknown value should return a result of
'Unknown'. In particular, observe that even 'null = null' evaluates to null.
So, what if we want to retrieve precisely those rows where the value of a
particular column is null ? Instead of testing for equality, we require a
different construct, as shown in the following example:

**Query 6**
SELECT day, fk_start_hour
FROM working_hours
WHERE fk_driver_id = 100
AND fk_route_id is null

### 6.2.2 Simple queries against multiple tables

Very often, the data relevant to a query are spread over more than one table.
Either the columns to be displayed are taken from different tables, or the
condition in the WHERE clause requires columns from different tables. In
either case, we can extend the form of SQL query given above, by allowing
a list of tables in the FROM clause. When this is done, all columns of each
of the listed tables become available for use in both the SELECT and
WHERE clauses. All rows which can be formed by concatenating one row
from each of the tables in the FROM clause, are potentially part of the
result unless eliminated by the condition in the WHERE clause. The

WHERE clause consequently has an additional function here. As well as
selecting the rows from individual tables (in relational algebra terms, the
*select* condition), the WHERE clause must specify which rows of the one
table should be paired with which rows of the other table (the *join*
condition). For example,

**Query 7**
SELECT licence_num, make, model
FROM van, van_type
WHERE fk_van_type = van_type_id
AND fk_base_loc = 15

This query can be implemented using select, project and join operations of
relational algebra. For example, the query processor might first select the
rows from van where fk_base_loc is 15, then join to van_type using
fk_van_type = van_type_id, and finally project onto the columns required
in the result.

In the examples given so far, we have identified columns simply by their
names. This is fine when the queries involve only a single table, but it can
lead to ambiguity when the query involves multiple tables which each have
a column of the same name. It is therefore necessary to allow an alternative
syntax, in which the column name is preceded by the name of the table to
which it belongs, with a dot ('.') separating the table name from the column
name. Since table names are often quite long, it is convenient to allow the
use of an alias for a table. The alias is introduced in the FROM clause thus:

SELECT column_list
FROM table1 alias1,  table2 alias2, ….
WHERE condition

The columns in the SELECT and WHERE clauses can now be referred to
using the syntax alias.column_name. For example,

**Query 8**
SELECT DISTINCT t.make,t.model
FROM van v, van_type t, location b
WHERE v.fk_van_type = t.van_type_id
AND v.fk_base_loc = b.loc_id
AND b.loc_name = 'Stoke'

With this syntax, it is also possible to express a query which joins a table to itself:

**Query 9**
```
SELECT r1.route_id,r2.route_id
FROM route r1, route r2
WHERE r1.fk_start_loc = r2.fk_start_loc
AND r1.fk_end_loc = r2.fk_end_loc
AND r1.distance < r2.distance
AND r1.weight_limit >= r2.weight_limit
AND r1.height_limit >= r2.height_limit
```

The above query identifies all pairs of routes, r1 and r2, between the same source and destination, such that r1 is both shorter than r2 and at least equally capable of carrying large vehicles (the height and weight limits being no smaller than those of r2).

### 6.2.3 Outer join

The join operation is sometimes referred to as a 'lossy' operation because a row from a given operand may not appear in the result of the join at all, unless it matches at least one row from the other operand. Very often this is exactly what we want from the query, but sometimes we may wish to include in the result those rows which do not have any matches. The outer join is a 'lossless' join operation, which preserves all rows of the operand, filling in the columns of the other operand with null values. Support for outer joins varies from one vendor to another. Some do not support them at all, while others (such as Oracle) allow only one-sided outer joins. A one-sided outer join preserves unmatched rows from one operand, but not from the other. In practice, this restriction is not so severe as it seems, because it is very often the case that we only need to preserve unmatched rows from one of the operands. The example below uses Oracle syntax to specify a one-sided outer join. The plus symbol ('+') is added in parentheses to the join condition, after the name of the column which is to be filled with null values when no match is found. For example,

**Query 10**
SELECT d.name, w.fk_start_hour, s.loc_name, e.loc_name
FROM driver d, working_hours w, route r, location s, location e
WHERE d.driver_id = w.fk_driver_id
AND w.day = '16-APR-2007'
AND w.fk_route_id = r.route_id(+)
AND r.fk_start_loc = s.loc_id
AND r.fk_end_loc = e.loc_id

Query 10 finds the names of all drivers who are working on 16 April 2007, along with the hours that they are scheduled to work. Where the driver has been assigned to a particular route for a given working hour, the names of the starting and ending locations of that route are also listed. Where the driver is due to work but has not currently been assigned to a route, the start and end locations will be null.

### 6.2.4 Order By

The order in which the results of a query appear is often unpredictable. It depends on the strategy which the query optimiser chooses for executing the query, and the way in which the rows of a table are ordered on disk. In general, a relational database system does not keep the rows of a table in a specific order. To begin with, it is very likely to store rows in the order in which they were inserted but, as rows are deleted and new ones inserted, memory becomes fragmented and the new rows will be placed where space is available. Sometimes the use of disk space becomes sufficiently inefficient that the rows need to be physically reorganised. At the same time, query optimisers have become sufficiently sophisticated that it is often hard to predict how a query will be processed. For example, there are several possible ways of executing a join of two tables. One way involves first sorting the operands, another involves using an index to quickly identify the matching rows. The strategy chosen is likely to have a considerable bearing on the ordering of the rows in the result. Yet very often we want to see the results of a query in a specific order. This requires the use of an 'ORDER BY' clause, which appears at the end of the query. The ORDER BY clause specifies that the results should be listed in order of the values of a particular column. By default ascending order is implied, but descending order can be specified instead by use of the keyword DESC following the column name. In the event of multiple rows having the same

130

value, the ordering of those rows can be controlled by including a secondary sorting criterion. For example,

**Query 11**
SELECT make, model,height
FROM van_type
ORDER BY height DESC

At this point, you may well be wondering what happens when the column in an ORDER BY clause contains null values. As stated above, the result of any comparison with null is undefined; consequently, the ordering of values is undefined whenever they include nulls. To get around this dilemma, we require an additional construct to specify that null values should appear either before or after all other values. We can write 'nulls first' after the name of a column to specify that null values should appear first in the ordering, and 'nulls last' to specify that they should appear at the end. For example,

**Query 12**
SELECT fk_driver_id, fk_route_id, fk_start_hour
FROM working_hours
WHERE day = '15-APR-2007'
ORDER BY fk_driver_id, fk_route_id NULLS LAST

### 6.2.5 SQL functions

The columns listed in the SELECT clause of a query often correspond exactly to columns in the database tables. In general, however, the SELECT clause can include expressions to generate columns of the result from those of the database tables. These expressions can be constants, arithmetic expressions or expressions involving functions. In particular, SQL supports a number of standard aggregate functions which act on a set of values and return a single value. These functions are COUNT, MAX, MIN, SUM and AVG: they compute the cardinality, largest value, smallest value, total value and mean value of the set, respectively. For example, query 13 computes the total distance of all routes to which the driver(s) named Fred Bloggs has been booked:

**Query 13**
SELECT SUM(r.distance) total_dist
FROM route r, booking b, driver d
WHERE r.route_id = b.fk_route_id
AND b.fk_driver_id = d.driver_id
AND d.name = 'Fred Bloggs'

Note that in query 13 we have introduced an alias total_dist in the SELECT clause. This is common practice when selecting a complex expression involving functions, rather than just a simple column. Without the alias, the result would have a column named 'SUM(r.distance)' which is probably not what we want. The use of aliases in such circumstances makes the form of the result rather easier to understand.

Query 14 computes the shortest distance among all routes from Stoke to Manchester:

**Query 14**
SELECT MIN(r.distance) min_dist
FROM route r, location s, location e
WHERE r.fk_start_loc = s.loc_id
AND r.fk_end_loc = e.loc_id
AND s.loc_name = 'Stoke'
AND e.loc_name = 'Manchester'

### 6.2.6 Group By and Having

So far, we have seen aggregate functions applied to all the rows of a table. Sometimes we want instead to compute an aggregate value separately for each of several groups of rows, where the groups are defined according to the value of a particular column. For example, we might want to compute the total number of hours on a certain date that each driver is scheduled to work but has no assignment as yet. We can obtain this information from the WORKING_HOURS table, by computing for each driver the sum of all periods on the specified date where no route has been assigned. The GROUP BY clause enables us to do this:

132

**Query 15**
SELECT w.fk_driver_id, SUM(end_hour – start_hour) free_hours
FROM working_hours w
WHERE w.day = '15-APR-2007'
AND w.fk_route_id is null
GROUP BY w.fk_driver_id

The query can be evaluated as follows. From the working_hours table, we select only those rows where the day is 15 April 2007 and fk_route_id is null (i.e., where the driver is scheduled to work, but no route is currently assigned to that driver). We then group the rows according to driver, find the duration of each period, and compute the total duration of those periods for each driver. Note that the effect of 'GROUP BY' is to create a set of groups, each group being in effect a set of rows. In other words, after evaluating 'GROUP BY' the result is a set of sets, and not a valid relation. This is fine, because we still have to evaluate the SELECT clause, which will create a valid relation (or table) from the set of sets. In order for this to work, it is necessary that the SELECT clause produces a single row from each group. In that way, we arrive at a set of rows as the final result, rather than a set of sets. This requires that some restrictions be placed on the SELECT clause whenever a GROUP BY clause is present. First of all, it should include all of the columns in the GROUP BY clause, so that we can identify the different groups in the result. Secondly, it can (and should) include one or more aggregate functions, since that was the reason for grouping in the first place. Thirdly, and most importantly, it must not include any other columns, because it cannot be guaranteed that such columns have a single value for each group.

Sometimes it happens that we don't wish to see all of the groups represented in the result. For example, in Query 15, we might want to see the results only for those drivers who have at least three hours of unallocated time available on that date. Queries of this kind can be handled by means of a HAVING clause. Whereas the WHERE clause is used to select from a set of rows, the HAVING clause is used to select from a set of groups. Thus, the HAVING clause is closely tied to the GROUP BY clause. It is perfectly valid to include GROUP BY without HAVING, but we cannot write a query with a HAVING clause unless it is preceded by a GROUP BY clause. The condition in the HAVING clause has similar restrictions to those imposed on the SELECT clause. In practice, though, the HAVING clause is almost invariably confined to aggregate functions.

Selections involving the columns in the GROUP BY clause are generally best placed in the WHERE clause. Thus, the example described above can be written as follows:

**Query 16**
SELECT w.fk_driver_id, SUM(end_hour – start_hour) free_hours
FROM working_hours w
WHERE w.day = '15-APR-2007'
AND w.fk_route_id is null
GROUP BY w.fk_driver_id
HAVING SUM(end_hour – start_hour) >= 3

So far, then, we have found queries with the following form:

SELECT column_list
FROM table_list
WHERE condition
GROUP BY column_list
HAVING condition
ORDER BY column_list

In this general form, only the SELECT and FROM clauses are actually required. Any combination of the other clauses can be included, except that GROUP BY must be present if HAVING is present. There is another important class of queries to be included, however, and these will be covered next.

### 6.2.7 Nested queries

A nested query is one in which a valid SQL query, enclosed in parentheses, is included within one of the clauses (usually the WHERE clause) of another query. The query in parentheses is called the inner query, and the containing query is called the outer query. In the simplest form, the inner query returns a single value and the outer query uses that value for comparisons in the same way that a literal value might be used. For example, the following query can be used to find the name of the location which is the base of driver number 55:

134

**Query 17**
SELECT loc_name
FROM location
WHERE loc_id = (
    SELECT fk_base_loc
    FROM driver
    WHERE driver_id = 55)

Note that the inner query is usually indented, to emphasise the distinction
between the inner and outer queries. The above query can be executed
efficiently by first evaluating the inner query and then using the result to
execute the outer query. Since driver_id is the primary key of the driver
table, we can be sure that the inner query returns only a single value (the
base location of a specific driver). The outer query then finds the one
location whose identifier is the result of the inner query.

Another example where the inner query always returns a single result is
where an aggregate function is used in the SELECT clause of the inner
query. For example, the following query finds the make and model of each
van type whose height is equal to the maximum height of all the van types:

**Query 18**
SELECT v.make, v.model
FROM van_type v
WHERE v.height = (
    SELECT MAX(v1.height)
    FROM van_type v1)

Again, this query can be very efficiently executed by first computing the
result of the inner query (a single value) and then using that result in
processing the outer query.

In other cases the inner query may return more than one value. For
example, suppose we want to find out the licence numbers of vans which
are based at locations in Stoke:

**Query 19**
SELECT fk_van_type
FROM van
WHERE fk_base_loc IN (

```
SELECT loc_id
FROM location
WHERE loc_name LIKE 'Stoke%')
```

The outer query uses the comparison operator IN because we are looking for vans whose location is one of a set of values. The database may contain details of locations named 'Stoke North'and 'Stoke South', for example. Note that the query can still be answered in a very similar way, first executing the inner query and then using the result as part of the outer query.

It is also possible to nest a query within the inner query. For example, the following query finds the distinct makes and models of vans based at locations in Stoke:

**Query 20**
```
SELECT DISTINCT make,model
FROM van_type
WHERE van_type_id IN (
    SELECT fk_van_type
    FROM van
    WHERE fk_base_loc IN (
        SELECT loc_id
        FROM location
        WHERE loc_name LIKE 'Stoke%'))
```

This query can be executed in three stages. First we find the locations whose names start with 'Stoke'; then we find the vans which are based at those locations; and finally we find the makes and models of those vans.

A more complicated class of nested queries is where the inner query refers to the outer query.In that case, it is not possible to execute the inner query first. Indeed, optimisation of this class of nested queries is considerably harder, and early relational optimisers did a poor job of it. However, such queries can be efficiently executed by modern relational engines. For example, we may wish to find the driver names and times on 20 April 2007 when the driver is assigned to a route for which neither the start location nor the end location is the driver's base. Thus,

**Query 21**
SELECT d.name, w.fk_start_hour
FROM driver d, working_hours w
WHERE d.driver_id = w.fk_driver_id
AND w.day = '20-APR-2007'
AND w.fk_route_id IN (
   SELECT r.route_id
   FROM route r
   WHERE r.fk_start_loc != d.fk_base_loc
   AND r.fk_end_loc != d.fk_base_loc)

In the above query, the inner query refers to the variable d which is in the scope of the outer query. Therefore, the inner query cannot be executed independently of the outer query. Instead, a three-way join could be performed between the driver, working_hours and route tables. Indeed, the query could be equivalently written in non-nested form, with all three tables listed in the same FROM clause. The reason for preferring the nested form here is largely one of clarity. We are selecting information only from the driver and working_hours tables, and the route table is only needed for expressing the condition in the WHERE clause: the nested form expresses this more naturally.

The nested queries considered so far have been expressed without introducing any new keywords. Let us now consider a further class of queries which does require a new keyword. Sometimes we wish to express a condition that a row with certain properties exists (or does not exist) in a particular table. In such cases, we don't need to retrieve any data from such a row, only to check whether or not it exists. We can do this by using the EXISTS keyword, which corresponds to the existential quantifier of predicate logic. For example, suppose we wish to find the vans which are not being used at all on a certain date. We can express the query in the following way:

**Query 22**
SELECT v.licence_num, t.make, t.model, l.loc_name
FROM van v, van_type t, location l
WHERE v.fk_van_type = t.van_type_id
AND v.fk_base_loc = l.loc_id
AND NOT EXISTS (
   SELECT null

FROM booking b
WHERE b.day = '20-APR-2007'
AND b.fk_licence_num = v.licence_num)

The construct 'NOT EXISTS' tends to be used more frequently than 'EXISTS' alone. This is because queries using 'EXISTS' can often be expressed in other ways, either through a nested query using IN or through a non-nested query with an explicit join. On the other hand, 'NOT EXISTS' allows us to express queries which would not otherwise be possible. Note also that the SELECT clause of the inner query selects only a constant (in this case 'null'). It really does not matter what we select from the row, since we only care whether or not it exists: selecting a constant removes the onus from the optimiser to detect that the row does not need to be fetched into memory.

The next example uses both 'EXISTS' and 'NOT EXISTS' for separate inner queries. In this case, we wish to find out which drivers are scheduled to work on a particular day but have not yet been assigned any routes for that day:

**Query 23**
SELECT d.driver_id, d.name
FROM driver d
WHERE NOT EXISTS (
    SELECT null
    FROM booking b
    WHERE b.fk_driver_id = d.driver_id
    AND b.day = '15-APR-2007')
AND EXISTS (
    SELECT null
    FROM working_hours w
    WHERE w.fk_driver_id = d.driver_id
    AND w.day = '15-APR-2007')

Although SQL does not explicitly include a universal quantifier, it is possible to express that construct by using two existential quantifiers, one nested inside the other. For example, let's suppose that we want to find out which vans have been booked for use for every working hour on a particular date. Another way of expressing that query is to find those vans

138

for which there does not exist a working hour on the given date for which no booking of that van exists. Thus,

**Query 24**
SELECT licence_num
FROM van v
WHERE NOT EXISTS (
    SELECT null
    FROM timeslot t
    WHERE NOT EXISTS (
        SELECT null
        FROM van_hours h
        WHERE  h.fk_licence_num = v.licence_num
        AND h.fk_start_hour <= t.hour
        AND h.fk_end_hour >= t.hour
        AND h.day = '20-APR-2007'))

### 6.2.8 Set operators in SQL

The set operators ($\cup$, $\cap$ and $-$) are supported directly in SQL, but are used infrequently in practice. Given two valid SQL queries whose results are union-compatible, the two can be combined using the keywords UNION, INTERSECT or MINUS as required. For example, suppose we want to find the routes which have been driven by both Fred Bloggs and Joe Smith. We can use the INTERSECT operator as follows:

**Query 25**
SELECT r.route_id rt_id, s.loc_name s_name, e.loc_name e_name
FROM booking b, driver d, route r, location s, location e
WHERE b.fk_driver_id = d.driver_id
AND b.fk_route_id = r.route_id
AND r.fk_start_loc = s.loc_id
AND r.fk_end_loc = e.loc_id
AND d.name = 'Fred Bloggs'
INTERSECT
SELECT r1.route_id rt_id, s1.loc_name s_name, e1.loc_name e_name
FROM booking b1, driver d1, route r1, location s1, location e1
WHERE b1.fk_driver_id = d1.driver_id
AND b1.fk_route_id = r1.route_id

AND r1.fk_start_loc = s1.loc_id
AND r1.fk_end_loc = e1.loc_id
AND d1.name = 'Joe Smith'

The INTERSECT operator always removes any duplicate values, so there is no need to use the DISTINCT keyword. Note that we could write similar queries using the UNION or MINUS operators:

- using UNION would give us all routes that have been driven by either Fred Bloggs or Joe Smith
- using MINUS would give us those routes which have been driven by Fred Bloggs and have not been driven by Joe Smith

In the case of UNION, there is an alternative form (UNION ALL) which retains duplicates. In certain circumstances, this can be a useful way of extracting additional information. For example, we might want to know how many times each route has been driven by each of the drivers, in which case the following query could be used:

**Query 26**
SELECT r.route_id rt_id, s.loc_name s_name, e.loc_name e_name, 'Fred' name
FROM booking b, driver d, route r, location s, location e
WHERE b.fk_driver_id = d.driver_id
AND b.fk_route_id = r.route_id
AND r.fk_start_loc = s.loc_id
AND r.fk_end_loc = e.loc_id
AND d.name = 'Fred Bloggs'
UNION ALL
SELECT r1.route_id rt_id, s1.loc_name s_name, e1.loc_name e_name, 'Joe' name
FROM booking b1, driver d1, route r1, location s1, location e1
WHERE b1.fk_driver_id = d1.driver_id
AND b1.fk_route_id = r1.route_id
AND r1.fk_start_loc = s1.loc_id
AND r1.fk_end_loc = e1.loc_id
AND d1.name = 'Joe Smith'

Sometimes, the set operators provide the most convenient way of expressing a particular query. Very often, however, a query which could use those operators can be more easily expressed in a different way.

## 6.3 Update statements in SQL

In addition to constructs for retrieving data from the database tables, SQL provides statements for modifying the content of the tables. Three different statement types are provided: INSERT, DELETE and UPDATE. The three are described in turn below.

### 6.3.1 Insert statement

The INSERT statement allows us to add new rows to an existing table. The statement begins by stating the name of the table, and listing the columns to which values are to be assigned. In its simplest form, the statement then provides a VALUES clause which lists the values to be assigned to those columns. The order of the values corresponds to the order in which the column names were listed. For example,

INSERT INTO working_hours(fk_driver_id, day, fk_start_hour, fk_end_hour, fk_route_id)
VALUES (100, '19-APR-2007', 9, 12, null)

This statement records the information that driver 100 will be working during the hours from 9 until 12 on 19 April 2007. The route is set to null, indicating that the driver has not yet been assigned a job for that period. If the statement executes successfully, it always results in a single row being added to a table. However, there are several potential pitfalls when using this form of the INSERT statement:

- there must be a one-to-one correspondence between the values listed and the columns to which they are to be added
- each value must be of the appropriate type for the column to which it is being added.
- the values must not be too large for the columns to which they are being added
- null values must not be inserted into columns which are constrained to be non-null
- if a unique constraint is defined on a column, the value to be added to that column must not be the same as that of an existing row in the table

- the values of any foreign key column must be either null or else equal to the value of the primary key of some row of the referenced table
- if a check constraint is defined on a column, the value added to that column must satisfy the check constraint

Sometimes the primary key column of a table is a counter which has no semantic meaning, such as the driver_id column in the driver table. In such cases, we do not want to specify the literal value to be inserted, but instead want to tell the system to take the next value from a sequence. This is accomplished by using the NEXTVAL property of the sequence:

INSERT INTO driver (driver_id,name,fk_base_loc)
VALUES (driver_id_seq.nextval, 'Fred Bloggs', 17)

As well as being simpler for the user, who does not need to know which values have already been assigned, the use of a sequence is also safer. Even if two insert requests are submitted at almost the same time, the database system will ensure that they obtain different values from the sequence.

The second form of the INSERT statement allows the result of a SQL query to be inserted into a table. In general, this results in zero or more rows being inserted if the statement executes successfully. For example, the following query records the information that all drivers will be working from 9 to 6 on 20 April 2007. This requires several rows to be added to the working_hours table.

INSERT INTO working_hours(fk_driver_id, day, fk_start_hour,
fk_end_hour, fk_route_id)
SELECT d.driver_id, '20-APR-2007', 9, 18, null
FROM driver d

Again, the same constraints must be satisfied by an insert statement based on a SQL query. A carefully written query can nevertheless guarantee to satisfy some types of constraint, regardless of the state of the database. For instance, the above query can never violate the foreign key constraint on fk_driver_id because the query explicitly selects the values from the referenced table.

142

### 6.3.2 Update statement

The update statement is used to modify the values of one or more columns for a specified set of rows. The rows affected are all those which satisfy a condition which is specified in the statement. The UPDATE statement includes a SET clause which specifies the new values to be assigned to specified columns, and a WHERE clause which specifies the rows to be modified. For example, the following statement can be used to record the information that driver 100 has changed his base to location 19.

```
UPDATE driver
SET fk_base_loc = 19
WHERE driver_id = 100
```

Since driver_id is the primary key of the driver table, this statement will update no more than one row. If there is no driver 19, the statement will not change the database at all. In general, though, the WHERE clause can involve any columns and can take any form allowed for the WHERE clause of a SELECT statement. Thus it can affect any number of rows. It can even include a nested query, as in the following example.

```
UPDATE working_hours w
SET w.fk_route_id = null
WHERE w.day = '16-APR-2007'
AND w.fk_route_id IN (
    SELECT r.route_id
    FROM route r
    WHERE r.fk_end_loc = 15)
```

The above statement sets all routes to null where drivers have been assigned to work on routes to location 15 on 16 April 2007.

As with the INSERT statement, an update will fail if any constraints are violated. The primary key constraint is rarely a problem for updates, because the primary key is usually an invariant property of an entity: it is rarely the case that we would want to modify the primary key value of a row. Otherwise, much the same issues arise with updates as with inserts.

When there is duplication of information in the database, it may be necessary to issue a second update statement to maintain consistency. For example, when we update the route assigned to a driver in the working_hours table, it is necessary to make a compensating update to the booking table.

### 6.3.3 Delete statement

The DELETE statement is used to delete rows from a table. Deletion of data is required when data have been entered erroneously, or when the data are no longer required. The latter case depends on the application. In some cases, it may be desirable to retain all historical data, while in other cases only current or recent data are of interest. For example, if a driver leaves the company, we might or might not want to delete data pertaining to the driver.

As with the UPDATE statement, a WHERE clause is used to specify which rows are affected.The first example records the information that driver 55 is not going to be working on 17 April 2007:

```
DELETE FROM working_hours
WHERE fk_driver_id = 55 AND day = '17-APR-2007'
```

As with other forms of SQL statement, the DELETE statement allows the use of an IN operator to express the condition that a value is one from a specified list. Thus, the following query records the information that driver 55 will be off on both 17 and 20 April.

```
DELETE FROM working_hours
WHERE fk_driver_id = 55 AND day IN ('17-APR-2007', '20-APR-2007')
```

As with INSERT and UPDATE statements, it is possible to include a nested query in the WHERE clause. The following statement removes all bookings on 20 April 2007 on routes which terminate at location 15.

```
DELETE FROM booking b
WHERE  b.fk_route_id IN (
    SELECT r.route_id
    FROM route r
    WHERE r.fk_end_loc = 15)
AND b.day = '20-APR-2007'
```

As with the INSERT and UPDATE statements, we must be careful to avoid violating any constraints. But since we are not adding any new values to the database, the issues are quite different. The most common problem with a DELETE is to attempt to remove a row which is being referenced by a foreign key from another table. For example, we cannot remove a driver if there are references to that driver in the booking and working_hours tables. There are two possible ways of dealing with this problem:

1) delete the dependent rows first, so that the original deletion can be carried out without violating any constraints, or
2) Update the dependent rows, so that they no longer hold references to the row which is to be deleted (typically, this involves setting the references to null)

In our example, the most likely solution is to delete the entries in working_hours and booking which refer to the driver whose record is to be removed. We cannot create null values in the fk_driver_id column of either table, since those columns are constrained to be non-null. It would be possible to substitute a different driver for some of the timeslots, but that is a less likely approach to take.

To see a situation where we would want to update the dependent rows, let us suppose that each location has a site representative, and that we decide to add a column 'fk_site_representative_id' to the location table. This column would hold the driver_id of the driver who is the representative for that location, and would be constrained to be a foreign key column. Now suppose one of the site representatives leaves the company, and we therefore want to delete that driver's record from the database. We are unable to delete the row from the driver table, because the location table holds a reference to that driver under fk_site_representative_id. Yet we do not want to delete the location, because the location still exists and we need to store data concerning it. Instead, we can set the value of fk_site_representative_id to null, thus removing the reference to the driver and allowing us to safely delete the driver row. Note that, even had we wanted to delete the location in this case, it would not have been possible to do so. The reason is that we have introduced a circular dependency into the database schema. The driver holds a reference to the location through fk_base_loc, and the location holds a reference to the driver through fk_site_representative_id. We need to break this circularity by setting the reference on one side to null, so that the row on the other side can be deleted.

# Chapter 7

# STORED PROCEDURES

In this chapter, we shall look at ways of storing database access procedures in the database itself. We saw in Chapter 5 how the efficient performance of the system depends to a great extent on keeping down the number of messages passed between client and server processes. This requires the applications to send coarse-grained requests to the database server, and the server to send more than one row at a time when the result of a request includes many rows. In order to support coarse-grained access, applications can be designed to use *stored procedures* rather than issuing individual SQL queries. A stored procedure is a program module which is stored in the database and compiled on the database server. It can include multiple SQL queries and updates within a computationally-complete programming language supporting variables, branches and loops. There are several important advantages in using stored procedures:

- Performance – if the procedure involves executing more than one query, the application only needs to send one request to the database server, and the server only sends one result back to the application. This can represent a significant reduction in the network traffic, making execution of the request faster and improving the overall performance of the system.
- Integrity – it sometimes happens that whenever an update is made to one table, a compensating update is required in another table. In such cases, it is better not to depend on each application to implement the logic to maintain consistency. If all applications call the same

procedure, the logic only needs to be implemented in one place and integrity is more easily maintained.

- Security – if an application supports a web interface, security is a particular concern. It is dangerous to allow web access to a database account which has unrestricted access to the database. If applications are allowed to access the database only through stored procedures, the security risk can be minimised.
- Adaptability to schema change – as the applications evolve, it is inevitable that the schema will undergo many revisions. When the schema changes, the database queries often need to undergo a corresponding change. When database queries are embedded in the application code, it can be quite difficult to search the code and find out where changes are required. Queries embedded in an application are just raw text which is interpreted when the application is run. A stored procedure, on the other hand, is compiled against the database schema. If changes to the schema have rendered the procedure invalid, the compiler will detect the problem and indicate what needs to be changed.
- Adaptability to a change of DBMS vendor – when a database is supporting internal applications, it is likely that the company is committed to a particular vendor. But when a product is built for use by different customers with different database systems, it is necessary to support interfaces to a range of database systems. This is non-trivial because each database system implements its own variant of SQL. Supported domains vary from one vendor to another, and the range and syntax of operations also varies. One approach would be to restrict the applications to using a subset of SQL which applies to more than one database vendor. The problem with that is that the application would not be making best use of the features of any one system. If performance is an important concern (as it usually is) the lowest-common-denominator approach will be unsatisfactory. It is better to accept that each database system will require a separate interface, and to build interfaces which are targeted at making best use of that database system's features. Stored procedures are well suited for that purpose. We have already stated that they can provide good performance; as for changing from one vendor to another, we simply need to rewrite each procedure in the language of the required vendor. The interfaces to the procedures should not need to change.

Most of the leading database systems (including Oracle, DB2 and SQL Server) support stored procedures, although each uses its own language for defining them. In this chapter, we shall describe PL/SQL, which is the language used by Oracle. However, similar principles apply to defining stored procedures for other database systems.

## 7.1 Oracle's PL/SQL

In PL/SQL the code is organised into *packages*, where each package contains a number of stored procedures or functions. As with other languages, the distinction between a function and a procedure is that the former computes a single result which is returned as the result of the function, while the latter carries out some operation (possibly involving updates to the database) and takes both input and output through parameters. The role of a package in PL/SQL is somewhat similar to that of a Java package. The full name of a procedure or function includes the package name at the beginning, as with Java, but it is possible to omit the package name when invoking another procedure or function within the same package. A package has a specification and a body: the specification defines the public interface, while the body defines the implementation of the procedures and functions. If a procedure is defined in the body but not in the specification, it can be accessed only by other procedures in the same package.

### Package interface definition

A package is loaded into the database from a file containing a script which defines the package. It is usual to have one file defining the public interface and another file containing the definition of the procedures. The public interface can be defined in the following way:

CREATE OR REPLACE PACKAGE my_package AS

--procedure signatures go here

END my_package;
/

148

The signature of a procedure includes its name, along with the name and type of each parameter. For example,

PROCEDURE store_submission (p_submitter_id IN VARCHAR2,
    p_xml_submission IN CLOB, p_return_code_o OUT INTEGER,
    p_error_message_o OUT VARCHAR2);

The above procedure has two input parameters. The first parameter, p_submitter_id, is of type VARCHAR2, which is Oracle's data type for strings of length 4000 or less; the second parameter, p_xml_submission, is of type CLOB, which is the data type for longer strings of characters. There are also two output parameters. The first out parameter, p_return_code_o, indicates whether or not the procedure completed its execution successfully. It is usual for a return code of 0 to indicate success, while a non-zero value can represent the Oracle code for a particular error type. Most Oracle error codes are negative integers, leaving positive integers available for user-defined error types if required. The final out parameter is used only in the event that a non-zero error code is returned. The value of p_error_message_o is to be a textual description of the error, in cases where execution did not complete successfully.

The signature of a function is similar to that of a procedure, but the return type must also be given. For example,

FUNCTION get_next_sequence_number (p_submitter_id IN VARCHAR2)
RETURNS INTEGER;

When the script is executed, the package interface definition gets loaded into the database. If the package is already defined, the previous definition will be dropped and replaced by the new one.

**Package body definition**

In a similar way, we can also create a script for defining the implementation of the procedures and functions:

CREATE OR REPLACE PACKAGE BODY my_package AS

--definitions go here

149

END my_package;
/

Each procedure or function consists of three basic blocks: declaration block, execution block and exception block.

**Declaration block**

The declaration block is used to declare variables which are local to that procedure. Each declaration consists of the variable name followed by its type. The declaration block can be initiated by the keyword 'DECLARE'. For example,

DECLARE
     v_total_cost NUMBER;
     v_department_name VARCHAR2(30);

In many cases, a variable is assigned a value by retrieving from a particular database column. Consequently, its type is required to be the same as that of the column. In order that the declaration will remain valid even when a schema change modifies the type of the column, it is often convenient to define a variable's type to be 'whatever type a certain column has'. Thus

DECLARE
     v_my_variable my_table.my_column%TYPE;

Sometimes it is necessary to execute a SQL query and process the result within a PL/SQL procedure. If the result is expected to contain more than one row, it is necessary to define a *cursor* to iterate over the rows of the result set. A cursor is a special type of variable which can be used to refer to the current row in the result of a specific query. It is declared as follows:

DECLARE
  CURSOR c IS
     --- SQL query expression goes here;

Sometimes it is useful to declare application-specific exceptions. These exceptions can be raised within the execution block when particular exception conditions arise. Defining a specific exception type allows us to handle those exceptions in a special way within the exceptions block.

```
DECLARE
    unexpected_problem EXCEPTION;
```

## Execution block

The execution block starts with the keyword BEGIN, and it is where the SQL queries and updates are carried out. When executing a query, the results can be assigned to local variables if required. For example,

```
SELECT my_column
INTO my_variable
FROM my_table
WHERE my_primary_key = 123;
```

In this example, the query is returning only a single row because we are testing for equality of a primary key value. Therefore, it is valid to assign the returned value to a variable, provided that the variable has the same type as the retrieved column. If we tried to do this using a query which returned more than one row, an exception would be raised. Similarly, if it turns out that the table has no row with the specified primary key value, a 'NO_DATA_FOUND' exception would be raised.

Local variables and output parameters can also be assigned values by direct assignment. Thus

```
p_error_code_o := -1;
v_total_cost := 0;
```

In the case of a function, a value must be returned. So the function must have at least one statement which specifies the value to be returned, such as:

```
RETURN 100;
```

Flow control is supported through conditional statements and loops. The structure of a conditional statement is as follows:

```
IF condition
THEN action
ELSE alternative_action
END IF;
```

As with other languages, the ELSE clause is optional. The action can itself include a conditional statement, making a nested 'IF'. The use of 'END IF' makes the parsing of nested conditionals clear and unambiguous. Thus

```
IF p_error_code_o != 0
THEN IF p_error_code_o < 0
        THEN p_ message_o := 'Negative error code returned';
        END IF;
ELSE p_message_o := 'Execution successful';
END IF;
```

The structure of a loop in PL/SQL is as follows:

```
LOOP
        --Some processing
END LOOP;
```

A familiar style of loop is the for-loop which can be used to execute a body of code a known number of times. A for-loop is written by specifying the range of the loop variable before the LOOP keyword.

```
FOR n IN 1..4
LOOP
        --- Some processing
END LOOP;
```

Another type of loop is useful, for example, when iterating over the result set of a query which returns several rows. When executing such a query, a cursor is used to keep track of the current row of the result. For example,

```
CURSOR c IS
    SELECT name
    FROM person
    WHERE job_title = 'Department Head';
```

Having defined the cursor, we can use a loop to fetch one row at a time. Thus

```
LOOP
    FETCH c INTO x
    EXIT WHEN c%NOTFOUND;
    --process the current row
END LOOP;
```

The FETCH statement retrieves the next row from the result into a local variable, so that it can be processed within the loop. The NOTFOUND check is useful as a means of terminating the loop when all rows have been processed. When all rows have been processed, the cursor should be closed:

```
CLOSE c;
```

It is sometimes useful to be able to raise an exception when a particular unexpected condition arises. Application-specific exceptions are typically raised in this way:

```
RAISE unexpected_problem;
```

The exception can then be handled within the exceptions block.

**Exceptions block**

The exception block begins with the keyword 'EXCEPTION', and is used to specify what should happen when an exception is thrown during the processing of the execution block. Specific actions can be specified for particular types of exception, or a catch-all can be defined for any types of exception which have not been explicitly listed. There are many different types of built-in exception which Oracle can raise, and there may also be application-specific exceptions which have been defined within the procedure. For example, suppose we want to treat a NO_DATA_FOUND exception in one way, and any other kind of exception in another way. This can be done as follows:

```
WHEN NO_DATA_FOUND THEN
    p_error_code_o := 1;
    p_exception_o := 'No matching row in table';
WHEN OTHERS THEN
    p_error_code_o :=  99;
    p_exception_o := 'An unexpected error occurred';
```

Oracle provides some useful functions for retrieving more details about the exceptions which it throws. SQLCODE can be used to obtain the Oracle error code, which is +100 for NO_DATA_FOUND and is a negative integer for any other type of pre-defined exception. Similarly, SQLERRM can be used to obtain the error message associated with that error code. It is usual to concatenate some application-specific text to the error message, to make it appropriate to the situation.

We now have the building blocks with which to build a PL/SQL package. In the next section, we shall look at developing such a package, and analyse some of the advantages which the use of stored procedures can bring.

## 7.2 Designing and using stored procedures

Having introduced the main building blocks of PL/SQL in the previous section, let us now take a look at an example. We shall use the database schema introduced at the end of Chapter 5, to develop a useful and fairly complex stored procedure. Recall that, in our example database, drivers first declared their working hours for a day, which resulted in a row being added to the working_hours table. In this row, the value of fk_start_hour would be the hour at which the driver is to start work, and the value of fk_end_hour would be the hour at which the driver is to finish work. The value of fk_route_id is always set to null in the first instance, because the driver has not been assigned to any route for that day. In the same way, a row is added to van_hours for each van which is available for use on the day. For example,

```
INSERT INTO working_hours (fk_driver_id, day, fk_start_hour,
    fk_end_hour, fk_route_id)
```

VALUES (10, '1-APR-2007', 9, 18, null);
INSERT INTO van_hours (fk_licence_num, day, fk_start_hour,
    fk_end_hour, fk_route_id)
VALUES (11, '1-APR-2007', 8, 20, null);

This records the information that driver 10 will be working from 9 A.M. to 6 P.M. on 1 April 2007, and that van 11 is available for use between 8 A.M. and 8 P.M. on the same day. Now suppose the company receives a request to make a delivery from location A to location B on 1 April 2007, using a van of a specified type. The system must allocate a time for the delivery, and assign a driver, van and route. The operation can be broken down into the following steps:

1) Find the best route between the two locations which is suitable for a van of the specified type. Determine the number of hours to be allowed for the journey.

2) Find a driver who is available for a block of time at least equal to the required journey time on the specified date.

3) Find a van of the required type which is available for a block of time at least equal to the required journey time on the specified date. Compute the interval for which both driver and van are available.

4) If the interval for which both driver and van are available is sufficient to complete the journey, we have found a suitable driver and van. The operation can be completed and a successful result returned to the user. If not, go back to step 3 and find the next available van. If no such van can be found, go back to step 2 and find the next available driver. If all potential drivers have been considered and no match has been found, we have to return an error saying that the request cannot be satisfied using that van type on that date. The user will then need to decide whether to request a different type of van or a different date for the delivery.

5) Assuming that a suitable van and driver have been found at step 4, we can now complete the operation. A new row is added to the booking table, specifying the driver, van, route and time of travel. More complex changes are required in the working_hours and van_hours tables. Where previously we had one row in each table, showing the driver/van as available for a period of time, we now require up to three rows in each table: there is a period of zero or more hours before the journey, when the driver/van is still available; the period when the driver and van are assigned to the journey; and a period of zero or more hours after the journey, when the driver/van becomes available again.

155

Clearly, no row needs to be added to represent a period of zero hours but, if the period is one hour or more, a new row must be added. So in general we are adding one row to the booking table; replacing one row of working_hours with between one and three new rows; and replacing one row of van_hours with between one and three new rows.

We are making a few simplifying assumptions in order to make the implementation of the operation reasonably straightforward. First of all, we are not going to worry about finding the best combination of van and driver for the job – as long as we can find a feasible combination, that will do. As a consequence, we may find that one driver is booked for all of his hours, while another has not been assigned a single journey. After all, our purpose here is to illustrate features of PL/SQL, not to come up with the ideal algorithm. Secondly, there is the question of whether the van and driver will be at the required location before the start of the journey, or whether they will need to travel there. Our assumption is that both drivers and vans are assigned only to journeys from their own base locations. At the end of the journey, the driver will bring the van back to the base location. The time required for the return journey will be factored in to the computed journey time. This approach may be criticised on efficiency grounds, but it helps to keep the implementation simple.

Now let us define the specification for a package which will initially contain just this one procedure:

```
CREATE OR REPLACE PACKAGE delivery_pck AS (

    PROCEDURE make_booking (
            p_van_make IN van_type.make%TYPE,
            p_van_model IN van_type.model%TYPE,
            p_start_loc_name IN location.loc_name%TYPE,
            p_end_loc_name IN location.loc_name%TYPE,
            p_day IN booking.day%TYPE,
            p_driver_name_o OUT driver.name%TYPE,
            p_licence_num_o OUT van.licence_num%TYPE,
            p_route_id_o OUT route.route_id%TYPE,
            p_error_code_o OUT INTEGER,
            p_exception_o OUT VARCHAR2);

END delivery_pck;
```

/

The operation requires the user to specify the make and model of the van, the names of the start and end locations, and the required date of delivery. The procedure will return an error code which indicates whether or not the operation was successful. In the event of success, the name of the assigned driver and the licence number of the van will be returned, along with the route chosen. In the event of an error, an exception string will be returned in addition to the error code.

We can now determine an outline of the procedure body, based on the five steps listed above. We shall fill in the details of the implementation as we go along.

```
CREATE OR REPLACE PACKAGE BODY delivery_pck AS (

    PROCEDURE make_booking (
            p_van_make IN van_type.make%TYPE,
            p_van_model IN van_type.model%TYPE,
            p_start_loc_name IN location.loc_name%TYPE,
            p_end_loc_name IN location.loc_name%TYPE,
            p_day IN booking.day%TYPE,
            p_driver_name_o OUT driver.name%TYPE,
            p_licence_num_o OUT van.licence_num%TYPE,
            p_route_id_o OUT route.route_id%TYPE,
            p_error_code_o OUT INTEGER,
            p_exception_o OUT VARCHAR2) IS

    --- declarations go here

    BEGIN

        --- now determine the route to be taken

        --- next determine the driver, van and start time

        --- update the database

    EXCEPTION
```

--- exceptions block goes here

   END make_booking;

END delivery_pck;
/

In the declarations section, we need to declare any local variables and application-specific exceptions. Numeric and string-valued variables are required to hold intermediate results retrieved from the database. Cursor variables are required for those queries where we need to iterate through the result set. In our case, we are going to need three cursors: one for the query which selects the route, a second for the query which selects a driver, and a third for the query which selects a van.

```
v_journey_time INTEGER; --- hours taken to complete round-trip journey
v_driver_id VARCHAR2(10); --- ID of driver
v_driver_name VARCHAR2(30); --- name of driver
v_start_hour INTEGER; --- start of period when driver is available
v_end_hour INTEGER; --- end of period when driver is available
v_licence_num VARCHAR2(10); --- licence number of van
v_van_start INTEGER; --- start of period when van is available
v_van_end INTEGER; --- end of period when van is available
v_journey_start INTEGER; --- time proposed for start of journey
v_journey_end INTEGER; --- time proposed for end of journey

--- query to select route
CURSOR route_cursor IS
    SELECT r.route_id, r.journey_time
    FROM route r, location s, location e, van_type v
    WHERE s.loc_name = p_start_loc_name
    AND e.loc_name = p_end_loc_name
    AND v.make = p_van_make
    AND v.model = p_van_model
    AND r.fk_start_loc = s.loc_id
    AND r.fk_end_loc = e.loc_id
    AND r.weight_limit >= v.weight
    AND r.height_limit >= v.height
    ORDER BY r.distance;
```

```
--- query to select driver
CURSOR driver_cursor IS
    SELECT d.driver_id, d.name, w.start_hour, w.end_hour
    FROM driver d, working_hours w
    WHERE w.day = p_day
    AND w.fk_route_id IS NULL
    AND w.end_hour – w.start_hour >= v_journey_time
    AND d.driver_id = w.fk_driver_id
    AND d.fk_base_loc = (SELECT loc_id
    FROM location
    WHERE loc_name = p_start_loc_name);

--- query to select van
CURSOR van_cursor IS
        SELECT v.licence_num, h.start_hour, h.end_hour
        FROM van v, van_hours h, van_type t
        WHERE v.licence_num = h.fk_licence_num
        AND v.fk_base_loc = (SELECT loc_id
                FROM location
                WHERE loc_name = p_start_loc_name)
        AND h.fk_route_id IS NULL
        AND h.day = p_day
        AND h.end_hour – h.start_hour >= v_journey_time
        AND h.end_hour – v_start_hour >= v_journey_time
        AND v_end_hour – h.start_hour >= v_journey_time
        AND v.fk_van_type = t.van_type_id
        AND t.make = p_van_make
        AND t.model = p_van_model;

--- exception indicating no route between selected locations suitable for
--- chosen van type
no_suitable_route EXCEPTION;

--- exception indicating no combination of van (of requested type)
--- and driver available on chosen date
no_resources_available EXCEPTION;
```

To select the most appropriate route for the journey, we need to find a route between the relevant locations which has a sufficient height limit and weight limit for the selected van type. If there are multiple routes which satisfy these requirements, then we shall pick the shortest of them. Therefore we can create a query which finds all potential routes, but returns the shortest first.

```
OPEN route_cursor;

FETCH route_cursor INTO p_route_id_o, v_journey_time;

IF route_cursor%NOTFOUND THEN
    CLOSE route_cursor;
    RAISE no_suitable_route;
END IF;

CLOSE route_cursor;
```

The query is a four-way join, in which the two joins between route and location are both equi-joins but that between route and van_type is a less common type of join. Note that, although it is usual to have an equality condition in a join, it is quite permissible to use an inequality as in this example. It is to be hoped that the database will contain at least one feasible route for each van type between each pair of locations. However, the procedure has to allow for the possibility that no such route exists. Therefore, we are raising an exception in the case that no suitable route is found. By using a specific type of exception for this case, we allow the exception-handling code to provide an appropriate response.

To determine the driver, van and start time we shall start by finding a potential driver. Then we iterate over the available vans until we find one for which a suitable block of time can be found. If no such van can be found for that driver, we need to try the same process for the next driver, continuing until either a match is found or there are no further drivers. Thus, we require a nested loop and two separate cursors (one for the driver and one for the van).

```
OPEN driver_cursor;
LOOP
    FETCH driver_cursor
    INTO v_driver_id, v_driver_name, v_start_hour, v_end_hour;
```

```
    IF driver_cursor%NOTFOUND THEN
        CLOSE driver_cursor;
        RAISE no_resources_available;
    END IF;

    --- now see if any vans are available

    OPEN van_cursor;
    LOOP
        FETCH van_cursor INTO v_licence_num, v_van_start, v_van_end;
        EXIT WHEN van_cursor%NOTFOUND;
    END LOOP;
END LOOP;

--- now assign the driver, van and time period

p_driver_name_o := v_driver_name;
p_licence_num_o := v_licence_num;
v_journey_start := MAX (v_van_start, v_start_hour);
v_journey_end := v_journey_start + v_journey_time;
```

In selecting the driver, we are searching only for those drivers who are
based at the location from which the journey is to start. We are also
searching for blocks of time on the specified day which are of sufficient
duration to complete the journey, and for which the driver is free. Note that
we may fetch more than one row for the same driver, if it turns out that the
driver is free for two or more disjoint blocks of time on the same day, each
block of time being sufficient for the journey. This is fine, because we need
to consider each block of time separately – if no van is available for the first
block of time, it is still possible that we may find a van for the second block
of time.

In selecting the van, we have a three-way join, because we need to consider
the van type as well as the times at which it is available. Since we already
know the hours for which the driver is available, we have added to the van
search a condition that the intersection of the van's availability with the
driver's availability should be sufficient to complete the journey.
Consequently, once we fetch the van, we know that we can find a feasible
block of time for that van and the driver.

To assign the time for the journey, we know that the earliest possible start time is the later of the time when the driver becomes available and the time when the van becomes available. So the journey starts at that time, and ends at a time which is computed by adding the duration of the journey to the start time.

Now let us look at the updating of the tables. Assuming that we got this far without raising an exception, we always need to insert a row into the booking table. For each of working_hours and van_hours, we replace one existing row with between one and three new rows. Our approach is to update the existing row with the values of the known new row, and use conditional statements to add the possible additional rows.

```
INSERT INTO booking (fk_driver_id, fk_licence_num, fk_route_id, day,
    start_hour, end_hour)
VALUES (v_driver_id, v_licence_num, p_route_id_o, p_day,
    v_journey_start, v_journey_end);

UPDATE working_hours
SET fk_route_id = p_route_id_o,
    fk_start_hour = v_journey_start,
    fk_end_hour = v_journey_end
WHERE fk_driver_id = v_driver_id
AND day = p_day
AND fk_start_hour = v_start_hour;

IF v_start_hour < v_journey_start THEN
    INSERT INTO working_hours (fk_driver_id, day, fk_start_hour,
        fk_end_hour, fk_route_id)
    VALUES (v_driver_id, p_day, v_start_hour, v_journey_start, NULL);
END IF;

IF v_journey_end < v_end_hour THEN
    INSERT INTO working_hours (fk_driver_id, day, fk_start_hour,
        fk_end_hour, fk_route_id)
    VALUES (v_driver_id, p_day, v_journey_end, v_end_hour, NULL);
END IF;
```

```
UPDATE van_hours
SET fk_route_id = p_route_id_o,
    fk_start_hour = v_journey_start,
    fk_end_hour = v_journey_end
WHERE fk_licence_num = v_licence_num
AND day = p_day
AND fk_start_hour = v_van_start;

IF v_van_start < v_journey_start THEN
    INSERT INTO van_hours (fk_licence_num, day, fk_start_hour,
        fk_end_hour, fk_route_id)
    VALUES (v_licence_num, p_day, v_van_start, v_journey_start,
NULL);
END IF;

IF v_journey_end < v_van_end THEN
    INSERT INTO van_hours (fk_licence_num, day, fk_start_hour,
        fk_end_hour, fk_route_id)
    VALUES (v_licence_num, p_day, v_journey_end, v_van_end, NULL);
END IF;

p_error_code_o := 0;
```

Note that, in both update statements, we are using the primary key value to select the row to be updated. In this way, we can be quite certain that only one row will be updated. It can be seen that the database update step is quite complicated, even though we are only making a single booking. This makes it much safer to have the updates done through a stored procedure, rather than allowing the tables to be updated individually which would make it harder to maintain the consistency of the data. Once all the updates have been made, we assign the error code of zero to indicate that the procedure completed successfully. We are going to return a non-zero code in the event of any error being encountered.

The exception handling block allows for each type of exception to be handled in a different way, if required. In our case, we have introduced two types of exception which are specific to this application and which therefore warrant special treatment. We are going to handle all other exceptions through a catch-all at the end.

```
EXCEPTION
    WHEN no_suitable_route THEN
        p_error_code_o := 1;
        p_exception_o := 'There is no route between the specified locations'
                || ' which is suitable for the chosen van type';

    WHEN no_resources_available THEN
        p_error_code_o := 2;
        p_exception_o := 'Unable to allocate a driver and van of the chosen'
                || ' type on the specified date. Please specify a different'
                || ' van type or different date';

    WHEN OTHERS THEN
        p_error_code_o := SQLCODE;
        p_exception_o := 'Error during processing of make_booking:' ||
                SQLERRM;
```

## 7.3 Transaction management

.When an application accesses the database through stored procedures, a key architectural decision is to decide where responsibility for transaction management should reside. One option is to control transactions entirely through the stored procedures themselves. In that case, any procedure which updates the database should execute an entire transaction. This means that, at the end of the execution block, the transaction should be committed. In the exception block, for any exception which constitutes an error, the transaction should be rolled back.

```
BEGIN
    --- various database updates carried out here
    COMMIT;
EXCEPTION
    --- exception handling here
    ROLLBACK;
```

Depending on the application, it may sometimes be preferable to give control over transactions to the calling application. The application can take a higher-level view, and can take into account factors other than the success or failure of a particular stored procedure call. In Chapter 9, we shall look

164

in detail at how to commit or rollback a transaction from within a Java application.

# Chapter 8

# ADVANCED QUERYING

---

In this chapter we shall look at extensions to SQL which enable us to express queries against more complex data types, and to express a wider range of queries against standard data types. Most of the main vendors support some of these features in one form or another, but there is considerable variation between them. Our presentation is based on the features provided by Oracle, since that is the leading relational database system at the present time.

## 8.1 Additional functions

In Chapter 6, we discussed the aggregate functions (MAX, MIN, SUM, COUNT and AVG) which have been standard features of SQL for many years. Each of those functions operates on a set of rows of a database table, and returns a single value as result. In this section, we shall look at a different class of functions: those which operate on a single row. Very frequently, it is useful to be able to transform the column values by means of a function, in order to derive a new value. This can be done in any of the clauses of a SQL query, such as the SELECT, WHERE and GROUP BY clauses. Oracle provides a large number of built-in functions, but we are only going to describe a few of the most useful ones here. In addition to describing specific functions, we shall also look at the performance implications of using functions. Use of functions greatly increases the expressive power of the language, but it is important to be aware also of the potential impact on performance.

### 8.1.1 UPPER and LOWER

The UPPER function is applied to a string, and has the effect of converting any lower-case letters to upper-case. Any other characters in the string are left unchanged. For example, suppose we want to display the names of locations (based on the schema introduced at the end of Chapter 5), and to ensure that all appear in upper-case. We could write the query as follows:

```
SELECT UPPER(loc_name)
FROM location
```

The LOWER function works in just the same way as UPPER, except that all letters are converted to lower-case.

### 8.1.2 Functions and performance

Now suppose we wish to see the names of drivers who are based at the location 'Stoke North'. We could write

```
SELECT UPPER(name)
FROM driver
WHERE fk_base_loc =
   (SELECT loc_id
    FROM location
    WHERE UPPER(loc_name) = 'STOKE NORTH')
```

If we are unsure of the case in which both driver names and location names are represented, we really need to use the UPPER function in both the SELECT clause of the outer query and the WHERE clause of the inner query. This is undesirable from a performance perspective, however, not only because we are applying a function a large number of times, but also because we may be preventing the optimiser from using an index. Let us suppose that the LOCATION table is very large, and we have decided to build an index on loc_name. If the WHERE clause is simply "WHERE loc_name = 'STOKE NORTH'", it will be possible to quickly find the relevant location by means of the index. Once we introduce a function into the WHERE clause, it becomes impossible to use the index because (in general) the system cannot easily determine which values of the column will map to a particular value when the function is applied.

A better approach is to make sure we know how the values are stored. This is most easily accomplished by enforcing the use of stored procedures for all updates to the database. In that way, we can quite easily ensure that all location names are in upper-case (for example) by applying the UPPER function to the name provided to the procedure, before storing the value in the table. Thus

```
v_upper_name := UPPER(p_name);
INSERT INTO LOCATION (...., loc_name, ....)
VALUES (..., v_upper_name, .....)
```

As long as we can be sure that all of the location names are stored in upper-case, there is no need to include the UPPER function in the WHERE clause of the above inner query. The system will then be able to use the index to find the relevant row very quickly.

It is rarely possible to use an index for the search when a function is applied to the index column in the WHERE clause. Exceptions are the MIN and MAX aggregate functions. Because of the way a B-tree index is organised (see Chapter 5) it is more efficient to find the MIN or MAX value of a column from the index than from the table itself, assuming that the table is sufficiently large to have justified building the index in the first place.

### 8.1.3 NVL

The NVL function is used to convert null values to a specified non-null value. In Oracle, a null is treated in the same way as the empty string, so a null value appears as a blank when the results of a query are displayed. NVL can be used to provide a more visible representation, where required. For example, to retrieve the working assignments of a particular driver (and displaying 'NONE' where the driver is due to be working but has not yet been assigned a route) we can write

```
SELECT day, fk_start_hour, NVL(fk_route_id, 'NONE')
FROM working_hours
WHERE fk_driver_id = 100
```

### 8.1.4 DECODE

The DECODE function is a particularly useful one, providing support for an IF...THEN...ELSE construct. The value of this is that it allows us to combine two or more queries into one, in such a way that the table need only be accessed once. If the queries were written separately, the table would need to be accessed repeatedly, which would be much less efficient. The general form of the function is

DECODE (expression, test1, res1, test2, res2, ...., testN, resN, defaultRes)

The expression is evaluated and compared with the various test values test1, test2, ..., testN. Where it finds a matching test value, the function returns the corresponding result res1, res2, ..., resN. If no matching test value is found, defaultRes is returned. The default can be omitted, in which case the function will return null in the event of no match.

As an example, let us consider that we need to calculate the pay for a driver according to the following schedule:

0.75/mile if driving a van of type A
0.60/mile if driving a van of type B
0.50/mile if driving a van of type C
0.40/mile if driving any other type of van

The query can be expressed as follows:

```
SELECT d.driver_id, d.name, b.day,
        DECODE(v.fk_van_type, 'A', 0.75*r.distance, 'B', 0.6*r.distance,
        'C', 0.5*r.distance, 0.4*r.distance)
FROM driver d, booking b, route r, van v
WHERE r.route_id = b.fk_route_id
AND b.fk_driver_id = d.driver_id
AND b.fk_licence_num = v.licence_num
```

The general form of the DECODE function can be interpreted approximately as

IF expression = test1 THEN res1
ELSE IF expression = test2 THEN res2
.........
ELSE IF expression = testN THEN resN
ELSE defaultRes

I describe this interpretation as approximate because there are complications with null values. Recall that SQL uses a three-valued logic in which 'NULL = NULL' evaluates to neither true nor false. Of course, we could always use the NVL function within the DECODE expression, to convert nulls to some specified string so that equality comparisons can be made. This would be rather inefficient and unnecessary, though, so Oracle implements DECODE in such a way that nulls can be compared for equality. If NULL appears as one of the test values, then a match occurs whenever the expression evaluates to null. As an example, suppose we want to find out the proportion of working hours that the drivers have been assigned delivery routes. To answer this, we need to obtain a count of the null and non-null entries in the fk_route_id column of the working_hours table. The query could be written as follows:

SELECT DECODE(fk_route_id,null,'null','not null') val, COUNT(*)
FROM working_hours
GROUP BY DECODE(fk_route_id,null,'null','not null');

## 8.1.5 TO_CHAR

Sometimes it is important to have some control over the formatting of numbers in the result of a query. For example, if the number represents an amount of money, we might wish to include a currency symbol; comma separators for thousands; and dot separators for cents or pence. The TO_CHAR function allows numbers to be converted to strings in accordance with a specified format. The general form is

TO_CHAR (number, format)

The format is a string in which '9' or '0' is used to indicate a digit of the number, and other characters can be included as literals. For example,

TO_CHAR (10952.50, '$99,999.99')

would return $10,952.50. If a number has magnitude less than 1, it will appear with leading spaces before the dot. If you want it to appear instead with a zero before the dot, a '0' should be included in the format string. Thus

TO_CHAR (0.50, '$99,990.99')

In Oracle, dates are also stored as numbers. The TO_CHAR function is used to convert dates to strings as well, but the format options are naturally different. An Oracle date is composed of year, month, day, hour, minute and second. They can be returned in any order, and in various formats. In addition, you can choose which of the components to return. Within the format string, the most commonly-used options are:

| YYYY | Year as four digits |
|---|---|
| MM | Month, 1-12 |
| MON | Month abbreviation, e.g., 'JAN' |
| MONTH | Month name, e.g., 'JANUARY' |
| DD | Day of month, 1-31 |
| DAY | Name of day, e.g., 'TUESDAY' |
| DY | Abbreviated name of day, e.g., 'TUE' |
| HH24 | Hour, 1-24 |
| HH | Hour, 1-12 |
| MI | Minute, 0-59 |
| SS | Second, 0-59 |
| AM (or PM) | 'AM' or 'PM', used in conjunction with HH |

The default format is DD-MON-YYYY. For any other format, the TO_CHAR function must be used. For example,

```
SELECT fk_driver_id, fk_start_hour,
       TO_CHAR(day, 'YYYY-MM-DD') date_of_work,
       TO_CHAR(day,'DAY') day_of_week
FROM working_hours
WHERE fk_driver_id = 101;
```

The TO_CHAR function can also be used in the WHERE clause. For example, we might wish to select only those rows pertaining to Mondays in July:

```
SELECT fk_driver_id, fk_start_hour, TO_CHAR(day, 'YYYY-MM-DD')
date_of_work
FROM working_hours
WHERE fk_driver_id = 101
AND TO_CHAR(day, 'DAY-MON') = 'MONDAY-JUL';
```

## 8.1.6 TO_DATE

The function TO_DATE is essentially the inverse of TO_CHAR when applied to dates. Whereas TO_CHAR will take a date and return a string of the desired format, TO_DATE will take a string and interpret it as a date according to the specified format. A restriction is that the format string should include all the date components, though the time part is optional. If the time is omitted, it defaults to midnight (0 hours, 0 minutes and 0 seconds). TO_DATE is most useful in INSERT or UPDATE statements, where the date value provided is not in the default format. For example

```
INSERT INTO my_table (my_id, my_date) VALUES ('001',
        TO_DATE('10-JAN-2007 11:30:00',
        'DD-MON-YYYY HH24:MI:SS'));
```

Note that, if the date is provided in the default format, there is no need to use TO_DATE. Oracle then allows us to write

```
INSERT INTO my_table (my_id, my_date) VALUES ('001',
        '10-JAN-2007');
```

The short form is convenient when we are only concerned about the date, and not the time. When the time needs to be specified, the TO_DATE function is required.

172

### 8.1.7 TO_NUMBER

The TO_NUMBER function is essentially the inverse of TO_CHAR when applied to numbers. It will take a string and interpret it as a number, according to the specified format. This is often useful in conjunction with another function, such as TO_CHAR or SUBSTR (see below), which extracts a part of a column value as a string. For example, we might want to select dates which are in the first six months of the year, regardless of the year. We can use TO_CHAR to extract the month, and then TO_NUMBER to convert the month to a number for comparison. The months need to be compared as numbers rather than strings, because string comparison has a different semantics. Thus,

```
SELECT my_date
FROM my_table
WHERE TO_NUMBER(TO_CHAR (my_date, 'MM'), '99') <= 6;
```

### 8.1.8 SUBSTR

The SUBSTR function is used to extract a substring from a given string. Its general form is

SUBSTR (string, startIndex, length)

The function returns a substring of the specified length, beginning at the given startIndex. Unlike in Java, the index of the first character is 1. Hence

SUBSTR ('Database Systems 101', 1, 8)

would return 'Database'. The 'length' parameter can be omitted, in which case the substring will be taken from the startIndex to the end of the string. For example,

SUBSTR ('Database Systems 101', 10)

would return 'Systems 101'. It is possible to specify a negative value for the startIndex. In that case, Oracle will count backwards from the end of the string. Thus

SUBSTR ('Database Systems 101', -3)

will return '101'.

### 8.1.9 TRANSLATE

The TRANSLATE function substitutes certain characters for certain other characters wherever they occur in a string. One situation where this is useful is when SQL is being used to generate a file in a special format where some characters have a specific meaning, for example, XML or Postscript. In XML, the characters '<' and '>' have a special meaning, so we would want to ensure that those characters are not introduced into an XML document as a result of querying the database. Thus, we might choose to replace each occurrence of '>' with '{', and each occurrence of '>' with '}'. This is easily done using the TRANSLATE function as follows:

TRANSLATE (myString, '<>', '{}');

The second and third parameters of TRANSLATE each consist of strings of characters. The characters in the second parameter are all distinct. The third parameter may contain duplicate characters, but it should be no longer than the second parameter. The TRANSLATE function will replace each occurrence of the nth character of the second parameter with the nth character of the third parameter. In the event of the third parameter having fewer than n characters, the nth character of the second parameter is simply removed from the string.

Another situation where we might want to use TRANSLATE is when we want to classify the values of a column. Suppose there is a table containing three types of entity, and the type can be deduced from the value of one of the columns. For the first type, the value of the column will start with a digit; for the second type, the value will start with an upper-case letter; and for the third type, the value will start with a character which is neither a digit nor an upper-case letter. We can deduce the type as follows: first use SUBSTR to extract the first character, then use TRANSLATE to map digits to '0' and upper-case letters to 'A'. The result will tell us the type. The query can be expressed as follows:

```
SELECT myString, DECODE(TRANSLATE(SUBSTR(myString,1,1),
        '0123456789ABCDEFGHIJKLMNOPQRSTUVWXYZ',
        '0000000000AAAAAAAAAAAAAAAAAAAAAAAAAA'),
        '0', 'Type 1', 'A', 'Type 2', 'Type 3')
FROM myTable
```

A third use of TRANSLATE is to define check constraints on a table. For example, suppose a particular column represents telephone numbers, and we want to constrain it to contain only digits, spaces and dashes. One way of specifying such a constraint is to remove those valid characters from the string, and check that the resulting string is empty. This is easily done using TRANSLATE:

```
TRANSLATE (phoneNumber, '0123456789 -', '') IS NULL
```

## 8.2 Storing and querying collections

Much of the success of the relational model can be attributed to its simplicity. There is only one type of data structure (the relation, or table) and each query acts on a collection of tables to produce another table as result. These features have facilitated the development of a simple yet powerful query language, SQL. At the same time, there is frequently a need to store data of complex structure, which do not naturally lend themselves to a tabular representation. Entities may have attributes whose values are collections, rather than simple values. While the relational model can represent such structures by the creation of additional tables, the representation is somewhat unnatural and makes query construction more laborious. In the 1990s, when object-oriented languages first became really popular, we saw the introduction of object-oriented database systems such as GemStone, ObjectStore, $O_2$ and Versant, which directly supported the storage of objects of complex structure. For a while, it appeared that these database systems would become an integral part of most object-oriented applications. That never really happened, partly due to problems with the object-oriented database systems themselves, and partly because it became easier to build object-oriented applications using a relational database system.

With the advent of Java, applications were able to integrate with relational databases through JDBC. This was a crucial development, both for establishing Java as a leading programming language and for ensuring that relational database systems would enhance their dominant position in the market. In addition, however, the relational database vendors took steps to make their products fit the object model a little more closely. One of those steps was to allow the creation of collection-valued attributes. By allowing an attribute to hold a collection of values, rather than only a single value, the relational model is able to represent information in a more natural way. The challenge is to extend the query language so that queries can still be expressed easily and processed efficiently.

Oracle supports two types of collection-valued attribute, the varray and the nested table. A varray is an ordered collection, which supports array-style access of elements. It is good for storing static collections and ordered collections of low cardinality. But when accessed using SQL, the whole varray must be fetched at once – it is not possible to specify a single element to be retrieved. Updating of a varray requires replacing one collection with another – you cannot add or delete elements from an existing collection. More flexible access to varrays is possible through PL/SQL, however. A nested table is suitable where ordering of the elements is not important. It allows for more flexible querying using SQL, to select a subset of the elements of the nested table.

Let us first look at defining a column to be of type varray. The first step is define a data type for the varray. This type must specify both the element type and the maximum number of elements. For example, suppose we have a table storing information about countries, and one of the columns is to hold a list of cities for each country. We might define a type as follows:

CREATE TYPE cityList AS varray(10) of varchar2(20);

This declaration defines the type cityList as an array of up to 10 cities, each of which is represented by a string of up to 20 characters. We do not necessarily need to store as many as ten cities for each country, but we shall not be able to store more. The table itself can be created as follows:

CREATE TABLE country (name varchar2 (20), population integer, cities cityList);

The table has three columns, of which the first two are of simple type and the third is a varray. To insert a row into the table, we need a way of creating a collection. This is done using a constructor-like syntax, in which we give the name of the data type followed (in parentheses) by the elements of the collection. For example,

INSERT INTO country
VALUES ('Italy',60000000, cityList('Milan','Rome','Venice','Florence'));

The country table can be queried like any other, except that the cities column cannot be used in the WHERE clause.

Now let us look at a slightly more complicated example, using a nested table. We are going to define the collection of cities as a nested table, and each city will have a population as well as a name. We begin by defining a data type for the an individual city:

CREATE TYPE city AS object (name varchar2(20), population integer);

The reserved word object is used to define a type with more than one attribute. Next we define a data type for the collection of cities:

CREATE TYPE cityList2 AS table of city;

The type cityList2 denotes a nested table, in which each element is itself of a complex type (consisting of name and population). We can now define the table of countries to have a column whose type is cityList2:

CREATE TABLE country2 (name varchar2(20), population integer,
    cities cityList2)
nested table cities STORE AS city2;

Note that, when a table contains a nested table, the create table statement requires a 'store as' clause. This is because, while a varray is usually stored within the same table, a nested table is stored in a separate table. Consequently, we need to specify the name of the table which will be used to store the nested table. This might seem like an inconvenience, but it is actually useful because, as we shall see shortly, it allows us to query the nested table much like any other. First let us insert a row into the country2 table:

```
INSERT INTO country2
VALUES ('Italy', 60000000,
    cityList2 (city('Milan',1300000),city('Rome',2500000),
        city('Venice',300000),city('Florence',400000))));
```

As with the varray, we create a nested table using the constructor-like syntax. In this case, the elements are themselves of complex type, so the elements are also created using a constructor-like syntax. The column cities thus contains a collection of four elements, each of which is a city with a name and a population.

Now suppose we want to add another city to the collection. Because we defined the column as a nested table, this is possible simply by inserting a new row into the nested table. This requires a way of accessing a nested table, which is done using the TABLE keyword. The TABLE keyword is used to indicate that a query which returns a single column is actually returning a nested table rather than a simple-valued column. Thus,

```
INSERT INTO TABLE
(SELECT cities FROM country2 WHERE name = 'Italy')
VALUES (City('Bologna', 500000));
```

Similarly, if we want to update the information regarding a particular city, we can define an UPDATE statement against the nested table:

```
UPDATE TABLE
(SELECT cities FROM country2 WHERE name = 'Italy')
SET population = 400000
WHERE name = 'Bologna';
```

Notice that the syntax, for both the INSERT statement and the UPDATE statement, is identical for nested tables and ordinary tables, except for the mechanism for specifying the table. The same applies to SELECT statements:

```
SELECT c.name, c.population
FROM TABLE (SELECT cities FROM country2 WHERE name = 'Italy') c
WHERE c.population > 500000;
```

Within the FROM clause, there is an inner query which selects a nested table (the cities of Italy). The outer query selects from this table just those cities whose population exceeds 500000. For our example, the result of the query is as follows:

```
NAME POPULATION
-------------------- ----------
Milan 1300000
Rome 2500000
```

These examples demonstrate that collection types can be used with little impact on the query language. This makes it possible to represent more complex structures within a single table. Collection types in a programming language, such as arrays, sets and bags, can thus be represented directly in the database. Nevertheless, many people prefer to limit their databases to conventional tables with simple data types. Either approach will work, the choice really depends on the priorities of each application.


## 8.3 Storing and querying large objects

Increasingly, there is a need to support storage of large objects in a database. On the one hand, there are applications which require access to large binary objects such as maps and photographs. On the other hand, there are many applications (especially web-based applications) which need to store and retrieve text documents, typically in XML format. Binary objects, of whatever size, require a special data type because none of the standard types will do. Text objects require a special data type if their size exceeds the maximum for the VARCHAR data type. In Oracle, the data type VARCHAR2 has a maximum length of 4000 bytes.

Oracle supports three main data types for managing large objects:
- BLOB represents a large binary object stored in the database
- CLOB represents a large character object stored in the database
- BFILE represents a large object (binary or character) stored in an operating system file outside the database

Large objects cannot be used for comparisons in the WHERE clause of a SQL query, in the way that other data types can. Instead, Oracle provides a package of procedures and functions which can be used in processing large objects. Functions, but not procedures, can be used in a SQL query. Both functions and procedures can be used in PL/SQL. In this section, we shall look at ways of using SQL and PL/SQL to store and query large objects. In Chapter 10, we shall investigate ways of passing large objects between SQL and Java using JDBC.

Let us start out by creating a table which can hold large objects in some of its columns. This requires no new syntax, all that is needed is to define the appropriate data types for the columns:

CREATE TABLE large_object_table (myid INTEGER, myclob CLOB, myblob BLOB);

The column myclob will hold large character objects, while the column myblob will hold large binary objects. Things become a little more complicated when we want to insert some data into this table. We cannot specify the values of large objects in the text of an INSERT statement, yet at the same time we should not insert null values for either a BLOB or a CLOB. Instead, we can begin by inserting empty objects into those columns:

INSERT INTO large_object_table VALUES (1, EMPTY_CLOB(), EMPTY_BLOB());

Having got an empty value into the database, it is possible to load the actual value from a file. In Chapter 10, we shall see how to do this using Java and JDBC. But here we look at how it can be accomplished using only PL/SQL.

Oracle provides a procedure called LOADFROMFILE in DBMS_LOB, to load a large object (either CLOB or BLOB) from an external file into the database. One of the arguments to that procedure is a BFILE representing the external file, so we first need to create a BFILE by specifying the name of the file and the directory in which it resides:

v_file := BFILENAME ('mydir', 'myfile');

Another argument to LOADFROMFILE is the number of bytes or characters to load from the file. Assuming that we wish to load the entire file, this value is easily obtained by using the function GETLENGTH. The PL/SQL procedure can therefore be written as follows:

```
DECLARE
    v_clob CLOB;
    v_file BFILE;
BEGIN
    INSERT INTO large_object_table (myid, myclob, myblob)
    VALUES (1, EMPTY_CLOB(), EMPTY_BLOB())
    RETURNING myclob INTO v_clob;

    v_file := BFILENAME ('mydir', 'myfile');

    DBMS_LOB.LOADFROMFILE (v_clob, v_file,
        DBMS_LOB.GETLENGTH(v_file));

    COMMIT;
END;
```

The package DBMS_LOB also provides functions and procedures for querying large objects. In practice, these tend to be more useful for CLOBs than for BLOBs. When accessing a binary object, we usually want to fetch the whole object, and it rarely happens that we need to search for a BLOB which satisfies a specific condition. A CLOB, on the other hand, is just a string, albeit one which is longer than most of the strings stored in databases. Very often, we will want to retrieve the entire object, but there are also occasions when it is useful to extract a part of the value, either to use in a search condition or in a database update. Searching based on CLOB values is not recommended as a frequent operation because of the performance implications, but it can be very useful when investigating problems in the database, or when performing data cleansing operations.

Let us suppose that a CLOB column is being used to store XML documents. One of the tags in the XML document is <empid>, indicating the employee identification number, and we decide that it would have been a good idea to have stored that value as a column in the database table. We can alter the table to add employee_id as an extra column, but we still need to find a way to populate that column for all the rows which have already been inserted. A straightforward way of doing that is to search each CLOB value for the <empid> tag, extract the value, and insert that value into the new column. To do that, we require functions to search for a particular pattern within a CLOB, and to extract a substring. Fortunately, DBMS_LOB provides functions to accomplish both of those things.

The function DBMS_LOB.INSTR will search for a given pattern within a CLOB. In its simplest form, it returns the index at which the first instance of the pattern appears within the CLOB:

```
v_startIndex := DBMS_LOB.INSTR (myclob, '<empid>');
```

Additional arguments can be provided to specify the offset from which to start searching, and which occurrence of the string to return (by default, it will start at the beginning and return the index of the first occurrence).

The function DBMS_LOB.SUBSTR will return a substring of a given CLOB, starting at a specific index and including a specified number of characters. For example, to extract the first ten characters from a CLOB:

```
v_substring := DBMS_LOB.SUBSTR (myclob, 10, 1);
```

Now let us see how these functions can be put together to update the table as described above. We first add the new column:

```
ALTER TABLE large_object_table ADD (empid VARCHAR2(9));
```

We are going to assume that employee identification numbers are always nine characters long. Within the XML document, we expect to find a string of the following form:

```
<empid>a nine-character string</empid>
```

We are also going to assume that the <empid> tag always appears once and only once within each document. To update the table, we need to locate the <empid> tag, then advance 7 characters to the start of the identifier itself, and extract the next nine characters. The resulting substring will be placed in the empid column. The UPDATE statement can therefore be written as follows:

```
UPDATE large_object_table
SET empid = DMBS_LOB.SUBSTR (myclob, 9,
        DBMS_LOB.INSTR (myclob, '<empid>') + 7);
```

This update statement will update each of the rows in the table. In some cases, a more selective update may be required, in which case the same functions could be used in the WHERE clause to help specify which rows should be updated.

# Chapter 9

# JAVA DATABASE CONNECTIVITY

We have seen in the earlier chapters how an application can make use of both Java and SQL to carry out different aspects of its processing. Java is good for handling interactions with the user, and for implementing the main application logic. SQL is good for interacting with the database. Both are very good at what they do, but they are very different languages, and the success of application development depends to a large extent on the ability to make them interoperate effectively.

One of the early developments in the Java language, and one which helped greatly in ensuring its early acceptance, was the definition of an interface called Java Database Connectivity (JDBC). The idea of JDBC was to provide a simple and consistent way for Java applications to connect to any SQL-based database. The provision of a uniform interface frees the application programmer from the need to know the details of connecting to a particular database system. On the face of it, it also means that a program written to access one kind of database can be deployed to access a different type of database without changing the code. In practice, however, this last advantage is seldom realised, for the following reasons:

- Although SQL is a standard language for relational database systems, different vendors implement their own dialects of the language. This means that some SQL statements will probably need to be rewritten if you switch from one database vendor to another.
- Some database vendors implement extensions to the basic SQL language, such as their own outer join implementation; special functions such as those discussed in Chapter 8; and support for

collection-valued attributes in a relation. If an application is designed to work unchanged with several different database systems, it will need to be restricted to use a 'lowest common denominator' subset of SQL. Although that is an approach that one can take, the consequence is that the application will not be making best use of the available features of a particular database system.

- Although JDBC is a complete interface definition, providing all the features that are required, some database vendors have implemented their own extensions to JDBC. This is done because the extensions provide a more efficient implementation than the standard interface. Again, it is possible to ignore the extensions and restrict the application to using the standard interface. But the consequence is that the application may not be making best use of the features of a specific database system.

In designing an application, therefore, it is important to decide at the outset whether the application needs to run against only one vendor's database system, or whether it needs to be able to connect to any. In the case of an in-house application, if the company has a commitment to a particular vendor and expects to continue with that vendor for the foreseeable future, it will probably make sense to design the application to make best use of that particular database system. If, on the other hand, the company anticipates changing to a different database system within the lifetime of the application, it becomes important to make the application flexible enough to allow a change of DBMS to be easily made. Similarly, if the company is building an application to sell to a variety of outside customers, and if those customers are liable to use different database systems, then flexibility is extremely important.

If the application needs to be capable of accessing more than one type of database, one approach is to try to make the code DBMS-independent, as far as possible. As indicated above, however, that is not generally the best approach to take, particularly if performance is an important consideration. A better approach is to separate the DBMS-dependent code into a distinct layer of code, so that it is possible to switch to a different database vendor by rewriting just that layer. One way of achieving that is by using stored procedures to access the database. Then, as long as the interface to the stored procedures is the same across all database systems, there is no need to change the application code at all. All that is needed is to rewrite the stored procedures in the language of the new DBMS.

In the remainder of this chapter, we shall examine the various aspects of JDBC, and describe an approach to building applications. But first we need to examine the software which supports the JDBC interface, by translating into calls to the underlying database system.

## 9.1 JDBC Drivers

Before we can contemplate developing an application using JDBC, it is necessary to have a *JDBC driver*. This is the software which implements the interface to a particular database management system, translating code from JDBC into calls to the underlying database system. Many different JDBC drivers exist for each of the leading relational database systems, and they are generally classified into four categories:

- A type 1 driver is a JDBC-ODBC bridge. This type of driver implements JDBC on top of ODBC (open database connectivity). ODBC is designed as an interface to database systems which is independent of any particular programming language as well as independent of any particular database system. A type 1 driver translates JDBC method invocations into ODBC calls, so that a two-stage translation is required. As a result, not only does it require an ODBC implementation to be present on the client machine, it also is likely to be the least efficient implementation. It really only makes sense to use a type 1 driver if no alternative is available, which should not be the case for any of the leading database systems.
- A type 2 driver is one which translates JDBC method invocations into calls to the client API of the underlying DBMS. An example is Oracle's OCI (Oracle call interface) driver. These drivers generally provide efficient implementations but they do require an implementation of the client API on each client machine.
- A type 3 driver is one which translates JDBC method invocations into a high level net protocol. Server software is responsible for the translation from this net protocol into calls to a specific DBMS. This type of driver has the advantage of not requiring additional software on the client machine, but the two-step translation process is liable to be somewhat inefficient.
- A type 4 driver translates directly from JDBC method invocations to calls to the underlying DBMS server. Like the type 3 driver, it is implemented entirely in Java and requires no additional software on the

client machine. It also has the potential to be the most efficient approach because it uses a one-step translation. If a good type 4 driver is available for the DBMS which you wish to use, it is likely to be the best choice. Examples include Oracle's thin driver.

The choice of a driver is not always straightforward, particularly if multiple vendors are offering the same type of driver. If in doubt as to which is the best driver to choose, it is best to carry out some performance evaluation, comparing the response times of different drivers when executing the same source code. When you have downloaded your chosen driver, you will need to add the relevant .zip file to your classpath. Within your Java program, you can then load the driver class as follows:

Class.forName("full.className.of.driver");

It is important to understand something of how your driver works, in order to make the most effective use of it. If this information is not readily available in the form of documentation, it may be necessary to spend some time running performance tests to see what works best. We shall look at performance issues later in this chapter, but first we shall look at the main constituents of the JDBC API. JDBC consists of a set of interfaces within the java.sql package (for core Java) and some additional interfaces within javax.sql (for enterprise Java).

## 9.2 Connecting to the database

Once you have a JDBC driver installed and loaded, the next step is to obtain a connection to the database: in JDBC, this means obtaining an instance of java.sql.Connection.. The traditional way of doing so is to use the java.sql.DriverManager class as follows:

Connection conn = DriverManager.getConnection (url);

Where 'url' specifies the database to which you wish to connect. The driver manager will select a driver from those which are currently loaded. If you have only loaded one driver, you can be sure which one it will choose. The format of the URL string is quite complex. It will typically specify the driver, the host and port of the database server, and the database name. For example,

```
DriverManager.getConnection
  ("jdbc.oracle.thin:@10.1.99.100:1521:mydb");
```

In this example, we are using Oracle's thin driver to connect to a database called 'mydb' through port 1521 at IP address 10.1.99.100. Something is still missing in this example – the user name and password with which to log in to the database. There are three distinct ways of specifying these. One way is to add them to the URL:

```
"jdbc.oracle.thin:@10.1.99.100:1521:mydb:user=fred;password=secret;"
```

Another way is to use a different form of getConnection, which has three separate parameters for URL, userName and password. And a third way is to create a Properties object to hold the userName and password, and pass the Properties object to getConnection.

```
Properties prop = new Properties();
prop.put("user", "fred");
prop.put("password", "secret");
String url = "jdbc.oracle.thin:@10.1.99.100:1521:mydb";
Connection conn = DriverManager.getConnection (url, prop);
```

The second (and generally preferred) way of obtaining a connection involves the use of the javax.sql.DataSource interface. A data source first registers itself with a naming service based on the Java Naming and Directory (JNDI) API. Typically, the creation and registration of the data source are done within a separate program, not the application which needs to access the database. When the data source is registered, it is assigned a logical name which can be used by the application which needs to access it. The advantage of this is that the database configuration information is not embedded within the application. Thus, a change to the configuration does not necessitate a change to the application. The application makes use of the javax.naming.Context interface, which is part of JNDI. A connection can then be obtained as follows:

```
Context context = new InitialContext();
DataSource ds = (DataSource)context.lookup("myDatabaseLogicalName");
Connection conn = ds.getConnection();
```

Another advantage of using DataSource is that it allows us to make use of pooled connections. For any long-running application which requires frequent access to the database, it is highly inefficient to create a new connection each time database access is required. For one thing, there is a significant overhead in creating a connection, and the application's performance will degrade if connections are frequently created and closed down again. Another problem is that the application can lose control over the number of connections that exist at a given time. If the database has too many open connections, its performance will suffer. A better approach for large applications is, therefore, to create a pool with a known number of connections, which can be shared by different users. When a session requires a database connection, it obtains one from the pool. When it has finished its database processing, it returns the connection to the pool so that it is available to other sessions.

If you are not using a connection pool, you will need to close the connection when processing is complete. This is done via the close() method of the Connection interface.

Connection conn;
.....
conn.close();

It is important to ensure that all connections are properly closed after use. Consequently, this step is best performed within a finally block.


## 9.3 Creating and executing statements

In order to execute SQL expressions against a database, it is necessary to obtain a Statement object. There are three interfaces within the java.sql package which can be used for this purpose. The simplest, java.sql.Statement, is used for executing a static SQL statement which may be a query, update or data definition statement. A statement is obtained from a currently open connection as follows:

Connection conn;
.....
Statement stmt = conn.createStatement();

A SQL expression can then be sent to the database server via the executeQuery() or executeUpdate() methods. The former is used to execute a SELECT query, and returns a ResultSet. A ResultSet is the JDBC representation for the collection of rows in the result of a query, as we shall discuss in detail later.

```
ResultSet rs = stmt.executeQuery (
        "SELECT route_id FROM route where fk_start_loc = 25");
```

The method executeUpdate() is used to execute an INSERT, DELETE, UPDATE or DDL statement, and returns an integer result. The result indicates the number of rows which were inserted/updated/deleted when a data manipulation statement is executed. Data definition statements always return zero.

```
int numRows = stmt.executeUpdate (
        "DELETE FROM route WHERE fk_start_loc = 25");
```

Sometimes we need to run the same SQL expression many times, but using different parameter values each time. For example, suppose we want to insert three rows into the Driver table. We could execute three separate statements:

```
stmt.executeUpdate (
    "INSERT INTO driver (driver_id, name, fk_base_loc)" +
    " VALUES (10, 'Fred Bloggs', 22)");
stmt.executeUpdate (
    "INSERT INTO driver (driver_id, name, fk_base_loc)" +
    " VALUES (11, 'Joe Smith', 25)");
stmt.executeUpdate (
    "INSERT INTO driver (driver_id, name, fk_base_loc)" +
    " VALUES (12, 'Jane Jones', 22)");
```

This will work, but is likely to be inefficient because the three statements each need to be compiled and run separately. Performance can be improved by creating a parameterised SQL statement which can be used for all three updates, by simply binding different parameter values in each case. The statement then needs to be compiled only once, and can be executed multiple times. This is made possible by the interface java.sql.PreparedStatement.

With a prepared statement, we begin by compiling a template SQL expression including one or more '?' symbols which serve as placeholders for the actual values. We then bind the actual values to the parameters, before executing the statement. In this way, we only compile the prepared statement once but can execute it many times, binding different parameter values each time.

```
PreparedStatement pstmt = conn.prepareStatement (
        "INSERT INTO driver (driver_id, name, fk_base_loc) "
        + "VALUES (?, ?, ?)");
pstmt.setInt (1, 10);
pstmt.setString (2, "Fred Bloggs");
pstmt.setInt (3, 22);
pstmt.executeUpdate ();
pstmt.setInt (1, 11);
pstmt.setString (2, "Joe Smith");
pstmt.setInt (3, 25);
pstmt.executeUpdate ();
pstmt.setInt (1, 12);
pstmt.setString (2, "Jane Jones");
pstmt.setInt (3, 22);
pstmt.executeUpdate ();
```

Note that, when setting the value of a parameter, we need to specify which parameter we are setting; the type of value; and the value to set. For example, setInt (1, 10) indicates that we are using an integer value (10) to assign the first parameter.

The third type of statement is a java.sql.CallableStatement, which is used when invoking a stored procedure. CallableStatement is a subinterface of PreparedStatement, and there are similarities in the way that the two are used. A CallableStatement also uses parameters, these being the parameters of the stored procedure. Stored procedures have both IN and OUT parameters, however, and the two need to be treated quite differently. The IN parameters are set in much the same way as for a prepared statement, using methods such as setInt() and setString(). The OUT parameters do not need to have a value set before the call, of course, but it is necessary to register them so that the system knows the number and types of OUT parameters that it can expect to find in the result. For example, let us consider the procedure make_booking which was described in Chapter 7. The interface to that procedure was defined as follows:

```
PROCEDURE make_booking (
    p_van_make IN van_type.make%TYPE,
    p_van_model IN van_type.model%TYPE,
    p_start_loc_name IN location.loc_name%TYPE,
    p_end_loc_name IN location.loc_name%TYPE,
    p_day IN booking.day%TYPE,
    p_driver_name_o OUT driver.name%TYPE,
    p_licence_num_o OUT van.licence_num%TYPE,
    p_route_id_o OUT route.route_id%TYPE,
    p_error_code_o OUT INTEGER,
    p_exception_o OUT VARCHAR2);
```

To prepare a call to that procedure, we can create a callable statement thus:

```
CallableStatement cstmt = conn.prepareCall (
        "call make_booking (?,?,?,?,?,?,?,?,?,?)");
```

This indicates that we are going to call a procedure called make_booking which has ten parameters. At this stage, it is unclear which of those parameters are IN parameters and which are OUT parameters. To set a value for an IN parameter, we follow essentially the same approach as for a prepared statement:

```
cstmt.setString (1, "Ford");
```

To register an OUT parameter, we need to specify its JDBC type. JDBC types are defined by the class java.sql.Types, and include VARCHAR for strings and INTEGER for integers. Thus, we can register the driver_name parameter in the following way:

```
cstmt.registerOutParameter (6, java.sql.Types.VARCHAR);
```

To execute the callable statement, we can simply use the executeUpdate () method:

```
cstmt.executeUpdate ();
```

When we execute a statement, of whatever kind, it returns a result. We next need to look at how to process the results which the statement returns.

## 9.4 Processing results

In the previous section, we described three ways of executing SQL commands against the database. First there was the execution of a SELECT query (through either a statement or a prepared statement), which returns a result set holding the collection of rows which match the query. Second there was the execution of an update statement (which again can be through either a statement or a prepared statement), which returns an integer indicating the number of rows affected by the execution of the statement. And thirdly there is the execution of a stored procedure, which returns results through various OUT parameters. In this section, we shall examine techniques for processing results in each of the three cases.

Processing a result set can be compared with the handling of cursors in PL/SQL, which we discussed in Chapter 7. As with a cursor, we can fetch one row at a time and process that row within the body of a loop. JDBC provides a particularly simple way of checking when the last row has been fetched. The next() method of the ResultSet interface will fetch the next row and return a boolean result: true if it succeeded in fetching a row, false if the end of the result set has been reached. This leads to a common pattern for processing result sets:

```
// assume the string sql holds the query to run
ResultSet rs = stmt.executeQuery (sql);
while (rs.next())
{
    // process the next row
}
```

The actual processing of a row generally involves extracting the values of the various columns. This is similar to the process for setting the values of IN parameters for a stored procedure call, except that this time we are getting rather than setting values. Where previously we used methods such as setInt() and setString(), now we require getInt() and getString(). Once again, the individual columns are accessed by their position in the result set.

```
String driverName = rs.getString (1);
int routeID = rs.getInt (2);
```

Now suppose we want to process the entire result set and build a collection of Java objects to hold the full result. We might start by defining a Java class whose instances will each represent a row of the result set. Prior to executing the query, we can create an empty collection which will be used to hold the result. Then, within the body of the loop, we can create a new instance of the class, assign its instance variables, and add it to the collection. For example,

```
Collection res = new ArrayList();
ResultSet rs = stmt.executeQuery (
    "SELECT g.road_name, g.direction, g.length" +
    " FROM route r, route_leg g" +
    " WHERE r.route_id = g.fk_route_id" +
    " AND r.route_id = 11" +
    " ORDER BY g.leg_num");
while (rs.next())
{
    String roadName = rs.getString(1);
    String direction = rs.getString(2);
    float length = rs.getFloat(3);
    JourneyLeg leg = new JourneyLeg (roadName, direction, length);
    res.add (leg);
}
// res now holds the result as a collection of JourneyLeg instances
```

When processing of the result set is complete, the result set should be closed. If you no longer need the statement, it too should be closed.

```
rs.close();
stmt.close();
```

In fact, closing the statement has the effect of also closing the result set. Nevertheless, it is good practice to release database resources as soon as possible when they are no longer required, so it can be beneficial to close the result set before you are ready to close the statement.

194

When an update statement is executed, it is not always necessary to check the result. However, there are times when it is important to know whether an update has actually made any changes to the database, and different actions may be needed according to the result. In that case, we might use a conditional statement such as the following:

```
int numRows = stmt.executeUpdate (
    "UPDATE driver SET name = 'Jane Smith' WHERE driver_id = 15");

if (numRows == 0)
{
    // take action when the update had no effect
}
else
{
    // take action when the update did change the database
}
```

Now let us examine how we can obtain the result from the execution of a stored procedure. Recall from the previous section that we registered each OUT parameter before calling the procedure. After making the call, we can retrieve the values of those OUT parameters in essentially the same way that we obtained values from a result set.

```
CallableStatement cstmt = conn.prepareCall (
        "call make_booking (?,?,?,?,?,?,?,?,?,?)");
cstmt.registerOutParameter (6, java.sql.Types.VARCHAR);
cstmt.registerOutParameter (7, java.sql.Types.VARCHAR);
cstmt.registerOutParameter (8, java.sql.Types.INTEGER);
cstmt.registerOutParameter (9, java.sql.Types.INTEGER);
cstmt.registerOutParameter (10, java.sql.Types.VARCHAR);
cstmt.executeUpdate ();
String driverName = cstmt.getString(6);
String licenceNum = cstmt.getString(7);
int routeID = cstmt.getInt(8);
int errorCode = cstmt.getInt(9);
String exception = cstmt.getString(10);
cstmt.close();
```

It can be seen from these examples that the techniques for invoking stored procedures are very similar to those for executing SQL statements. In both cases the interface is straightforward, and independent of the specific underlying database management system.

## 9.5 Using metadata

In the majority of cases, the structure of a query is known in advance and is the same each time the program is executed. The query might be parameterised so that the condition in the WHERE clause depends on user input, but the result set will anyway contain the same columns. Occasionally, however, there is an application which requires the whole query to be constructed dynamically. Consider, for example, a generic reporting tool which allows the user to browse the database schema and select data from whichever tables he or she wishes. In that case, there is no way to predict in advance the number and types of columns in the result set. The application will need instead to query the database system to discover the type of each column, in order that it can process the result set correctly. This is made possible by the interface java.sql.ResultSetMetaData, which also provides a number of other useful methods.

To obtain an instance of ResultSetMetaData, it is only necessary to invoke the appropriate method on the result set.

```
String sql;
Statement stmt;
....
ResultSet rs = stmt.executeQuery (sql);
ResultSetMetaData rsmd = rs.getMetaData ();
```

If the number of columns in the result set is unknown, we can discover it as follows:

```
int numColumns = rsmd.getColumnCount();
```

It is then straightforward to construct a loop in which the columns of the result set are processed in turn:

```
for (int i=1; i <= rsmd.getColumnCount(); i++)
{
    // obtain metadata regarding column i if result set
}
```

One of the most useful methods for obtaining details of a particular column is getColumnType(), which returns the SQL type of the column. The result is an integer value, the result of mapping the actual data type to its nearest equivalent in java.sql.Types. The class java.sql.Types defines constant integer values for such types as VARCHAR, INTEGER, DATE, BLOB, JAVA_OBJECT as well as various others. As an alternative to getColumnType(), you can use the method getColumnTypeName() to return the database-specific type name as a string.

```
int typeValue = rsmd.getColumnType (i);
String typeName = rsmd.getColumnTypeName (i);
```

Obtaining the column type is sufficient to tell us whether the column value should be retrieved using getInt(), getString(), getFloat(), etc. Nevertheless, we may sometimes require additional information. For example, when processing a VARCHAR column, it may be important to know the maximum size of the column. For this purpose, we can use the method getColumnDisplaySize():

```
if (typeValue == Types.VARCHAR)
{
        int maxLength = rsmd.getColumnDisplaySize (i);
        // further processing
}
```

For numeric types, it can be useful to know the maximum number of decimal digits allowed in the column's values. This is obtained by using the getPrecision() method. In the case of floating point types, the method getScale() is used to obtain the number of digits to the right of the decimal point.

```
if (typeValue == Types.FLOAT || typeValue == Types.REAL ||
        typeValue == Types.DOUBLE || typeValue == Types.DECIMAL)
{
    int maxDigits = rsmd.getPrecision (i);
```

```
        int afterDecimalPoint = rsmd.getScale (i);
}
```

It may also be useful to obtain the column name, if it is not already known. There are two methods provided for this purpose: getColumnName() which returns the actual name of the column, and getColumnLabel() which returns the suggested display name. Some drivers implement the two methods to return the same value, but there is no rule as to what getColumnLabel() should actually return. Some experimentation may be needed in order to discover how a particular driver has implemented it.

## 9.6 Handling exceptions

Up to now, none of the code samples provided in this chapter have included any exception handling. In fact, most of the methods which we have described are capable of throwing exceptions which are instances of java.sql.SQLException. Consequently, almost any method which you write to access the database must either catch and handle a SQLException or else include 'throws SQLException' as part of its signature. This applies whether you are connecting to the database, creating a statement, executing a query, invoking a stored procedure or accessing metadata.

Exception handling is a very important aspect of any object-oriented application, and one of the most difficult aspects to get right. In most cases, a message of some kind will need to be delivered to the end user. If the problem is serious, and particularly if it is caused by a problem with either the application code or the database, it is likely that the error will need to be logged so that the application support staff can look into it and resolve the problem. But the message to be written to the error log is likely to be very different from the one returned to the user. If the user has made a mistake, such as omitting some information which is required, then they should be given clear instructions as to how they can rectify the problem. If, on the other hand, the system fails because the database is down or has run out of memory, the user should see a simple message to indicate that the system is currently unavailable. Requirements for the error log are quite different. Information should be detailed and verbose, but carefully targeted to real problems. Support staff do not need to see pages of information regarding erroneous submissions from the users, but they do need as much detail as possible when unexpected behaviour suggests a bug in the application or a

198

problem with the database. Stack traces and database error codes, which have little interest to an end user, are often crucial to support staff.

The need for different types of error handling will often make it worthwhile to create a hierarchy of application-specific exception types. Thus, when the original SQLException is caught, the error may be logged and another exception thrown. This other exception will be caught at a higher level in the application's method-calling chain, at which point another log entry may be written and a message generated for the user. The first level of exception-handling might look something like this:

```
catch (SQLException se)
{
    // add some code to log the error here
    throw new MySpecialException (se);
}
```

Various information can be obtained from a SQLException to aid in handling the exception. First of all, there are the methods inherited from java.lang.Exception, which apply to handling exceptions of any kind. Thus, for example, we might provide the following type of exception handling:

```
catch (SQLException se)
{
    System.out.println (se.getMessage());
    se.printStackTrace();
}
```

In addition, there are methods which are specific to SQLException, and which offer additional information regarding database-related exceptions. These methods provide the database-specific error code, and the SQL state, which are useful in diagnosing and correcting possible bugs in the application.

```
catch (SQLException se)
{
    int errorCode = se.getErrorCode();
    String sqlState = se.getSQLState();
    System.out.println ("Caught an exception with code "+errorCode+
            " and state "+sqlState);
```

199

```
}
```

Whereas an error code has a meaning only within the context of a specific database system, a SQL State provides a standardised, vendor-independent categorisation of the error. Consequently, it is possible to write DBMS-independent application code which includes specific handling for particular kinds of error. A complication is that there are two different standards for SQLState, one being X/OPEN and the other being SQL 99. Some drivers may return SQL state values based on X/OPEN, while others use SQL 99. You can find out which standard is followed by your driver as follows:

```
int sqlStateType = java.sql.DatabaseMetaData.getSQLStateType();
```

The static method getSQLStateType() returns one of two integer values:

- DatabaseMetaData.sqlStateSQL99 if the SQL 99 standard is used
- DatabaseMetaData.sqlStateXOpen if the X/OPEN standard is used

The existence of two different standards makes it difficult to write vendor-neutral code with special handling for particular exception types. It would be necessary to provide code for both standards, with switches based on the result returned by getSQLStateType().

When exceptions are thrown, the normal path of execution is not followed, and a consequence is that resources may be left open which would normally have been closed. When accessing a database, it is important to close statements and result sets when they are no longer needed. Connections should either be closed or (if connection pooling is being used) returned to the pool so that they are available to other sessions. The best way to ensure that resources are always tidied up correctly is to make use of the finally clause, because that it always executed, regardless of whether or not an exception is thrown. For example, consider a method to execute a SQL query which is known to return a single row with a single string-valued column:

```
public String runSQL (String sql, Connection conn)
{
    Statement stmt = null;
    try
```

```
        {
            stmt = conn.createStatement ();
            ResultSet rs = stmt.executeQuery (sql);
            if (rs.next())
                return  rs.getString(1);
            else
                throw new DataNotFoundException (
                                "No matching row for: "+sql);
        }
        catch (Exception ex)
        {
            System.out.println ("Unexpected error: "+ex.getMessage());
                        ex.printStackTrace();
        }
        finally
        {
            try
            {
                if (stmt != null)
                    stmt.close(); // this will also close the result set
            }
            catch (Exception e)
            {
                System.out.println ("Failed to close statement");
            }
        }
    }
```

Note that, since the attempt to close resources can also throw an exception, we need to include a try-catch block within the finally clause. Since the stmt variable is being used within the finally clause, it is necessary to declare the variable before the start of the initial try block, so that it is still in scope.

## 9.7 Transaction management

When the application is updating the database as well as retrieving data, it is necessary to decide at what point the updates should be committed to the database. A transaction can be committed by invoking the commit() method on the Connection interface, and rolled back by invoking the rollback() method on the same interface. In a typical interaction, you might want to define a method which executes a complete transaction, with a commit() at the end of the try block, and a rollback in the catch block. The following simple example runs a single update statement as a transaction:

```java
public void runUpdate (String sql, Connection conn)
{
    Statement stmt = null;
    try
    {
        stmt = conn.createStatement ();
        stmt.executeUpdate (sql);
    }
    catch (Exception ex)
    {
        System.out.println ("Unexpected error: "+ex.getMessage());
                ex.printStackTrace();
        try
        {
          conn.rollback();
        }
        catch (Exception ex1)
        {
          System.out.println ("Failed to roll back transaction");
        }
    }
    finally
    {
        try
        {
            if (stmt != null)
                stmt.close();
        }
        catch (Exception e)
        {
            System.out.println ("Failed to close statement");
        }
    }
}
```

JDBC supports an operating mode in which transactions are committed automatically. However, this mode is seldom appropriate for real applications in which it is important to maintain control over transaction management. To disable the auto-commit mode, simply execute the following statement on each connection:

```
Connection conn;
.....
conn.setAutoCommit (false);
```

There is one situation in which you may not need to issue commit() commands on your database connections. That is where you decide to use stored procedures for all database access, and to delegate responsibility for transaction management to the stored procedures themselves. The commit and rollback statements will then be placed inside the stored procedures, rather than in the Java code.

## 9.8 Performance tuning

Performance is usually an important consideration for applications which make extensive use of a database. Various steps can be taken to ensure that the application runs as efficiently as possible, and that database access does not become a bottleneck. Some of these steps involve the database only, while others address the interface between Java and the database:

- *Minimise the number of connections made.* There is significant overhead in establishing a connection to the database. Rather than repeatedly opening and closing connections, it is best to reuse existing connections as far as possible. Connections should be pooled, so that they can be shared between sessions. A session then acquires an available connection when it needs one, performs its database processing, and returns the connection to the pool.
- *Minimise the number of messages passed between the application and the database server.* Client and server processes usually run on different machines, connected by a network. As a result, there is a significant overhead in passing each message between the application and the database. To reduce the overhead, the application should request large units of processing at one time. The best way to achieve

this goal is to access the database via stored procedures, each of which can execute a number of SQL statements.

- *Use buffering of results.* This is really another aspect of the previous point. When processing a result set, the application may invoke the next() method a very large number of times. If each call to next() causes the server to send one more row to the client, processing of a large result will be extremely slow. If a statement is expected to return a large number of rows, it is worth giving the JDBC driver a hint as to how many rows it should fetch at a time. This is done by invoking the setFetchSize() method on the Statement object, e.g., stmt.setFetchSize(20). The actual number of rows fetched depends on the particular driver's implementation. Some experimentation will be needed in order to determine the effect of setFetchSize() on a particular driver.

- *Make full use of the language features and JDBC extensions offered by the database system.* The leading database system vendors offer non-standard features which increase the power of the query language. They also provide non-standard extensions to JDBC, which tend to be more efficiently implemented on their database systems. If portability between vendors is not a big issue for your application, significant performance benefits can be obtained by making use of these non-standard features.

- *Design the database so that the important queries will run fast.* Tuning the application will be of limited benefit if the database itself is poorly designed. Queries, especially those which are frequently executed, must be fast to execute. Joins of large tables are a common source of inefficiency, as are selections from very large tables. Where these operations are required, it is important to have suitable indexes defined, so that the operations can be performed efficiently. Another aspect of this is that the SQL must be well-written. SQL is a language which supports many ways of writing the same logical query, yet there is no reason to suppose that an optimiser will choose the same query plan regardless of how the query is written.

- *Use prepared statements where the same SQL will be repeatedly executed.* Rather than using separate statements to execute several SQL statements which differ only in the values of certain constants, a prepared statement can be used to handle all of the statements. This ensures that the statement only needs to be compiled and executed once, and the same query plan can be reused each time.

- *Make use of batch execution of updates.* When you need to execute a number of updates in succession, all within the same transaction, it is possible to send them all to the database server at the same time. In this way, only one request is sent by the client, and only one response message is returned by the server. For each of the updates, we first need to execute stmt.addBatch (sql). This enables the Statement object to build up a collection of SQL strings which make up the current batch. Once all of them have been added, we execute stmt.executeBatch (), which sends the whole batch to the database server. The result is returned as an array of int values, representing the return values from execution of the various update statements. Recall from Section 9.3 that the result of executing an update statement is an integer, corresponding to the number of rows affected by the update. The statements in a batch are executed in the order in which they were added to the batch, and their results are returned in the same order. A complication arises if one of the statements throws an exception, in which case drivers can implement either of two options. One option is for the batch update to throw an instance of java.sql.BatchUpdateException (a subclass of SQLException), as soon as any of the updates fails. The other option is for the batch update to continue processing the remaining updates in the batch, and to return a value of Statement.EXECUTE_FAILED (-3) in the position in the array which holds the result of a failed statement. Some experimentation may be required in order to discover how a particular driver deals with exceptions. It is also possible that a driver will not implement batch updates at all, since they are defined to be optional in the JDBC specification.
- *Choose the transaction isolation level that is appropriate for your application.* If serialisability is not necessary for your application, performance gains can be achieved by allowing a lower level of isolation. The interface java.sql.Connection includes a method setTransactionIsolation() which supports resetting the isolation level for a particular database connection. The method takes a parameter whose allowed values are Connection.TRANSACTION_SERIALIZABLE, Connection.TRANSACTION_REPEATABLE_READ, Connection.TRANSACTION_READ_COMMITTED and Connection.TRANSACTION_READ_UNCOMMITTED. The driver will attempt to change the isolation level to the one specified, though there is no guarantee in general that it will be successful (some isolation levels are not supported by all vendors).

Performance tuning also requires an understanding of the particular JDBC driver which you are using. JDBC is only an interface, and its implementation can vary greatly from one driver to another. An approach which works well for one driver may be less effective for another.

# Chapter 10

# ACCESSING COLLECTIONS AND LARGE OBJECTS FROM JAVA

---

The techniques for accessing the simple data types (strings, numbers, dates) through JDBC are very similar. Things get a little more complicated when we need to access collections or large objects. In the case of large objects, the complication is largely due to the sheer volume of data to be transferred between the Java environment and the database environment, while for collections there is the complexity of the data structures to be considered. Moreover, the various DBMS products vary in the scope and design of their support for these data types so, although JDBC does provide a complete interface specification, it is sometimes necessary to diverge from the JDBC standard in order to make use of specific features provided by a certain DBMS. In this chapter we shall present solutions for the Oracle DBMS. As far as possible, however, we shall follow an approach based on the standard JDBC interface. Consequently, only slight modifications should be required in order to make our solutions work on other systems.

In addition to the features of the JDBC standard introduced in the previous chapter, we shall make use of a further five interfaces from that standard:

- java.sql.Array is the interface representing the SQL type ARRAY
- java.sql.Struct is the standard mapping for SQL types, in which the Struct contains one value for each attribute that the type represents
- java.sql.SQLData is the interface for converting between instances of a Java class and those of a corresponding SQL type

- java.sql.Clob represents a large character object in the database, and is usually implemented as a logical pointer to the data
- java.sql.Blob represents a large binary object in the database, and is usually implemented as a logical pointer to the data.

We shall begin by looking at techniques for storing and retrieving collections, and will then go on to look at approaches for handling large objects.

## 10.1 Accessing collections from Java

As we saw earlier, Oracle can support collection-valued attributes via VARRAYs or nested tables. On the Java side, we can represent the collection-valued attribute as an array. In order to store the array in the database, we need to pass it to Oracle and have it converted to a VARRAY or nested table as appropriate. The appropriate data type will need to have been previously defined in Oracle, so that the conversion can be done correctly. As a first example, let us consider a collection of strings.

## 10.1.1 Oracle definitions for "array of strings" domain

Suppose we want to store information about countries. One of the attributes is to be a list of the major cities in the country. Such a list could be stored as a VARRAY, but first we need to define a named type:

```
create type cityList as varray(10) of varchar2(20);
```

Having created the type, we can define the table to include a column whose domain is that type:

```
create table country (name varchar2 (20), population integer, cities cityList);
```

We shall now present ways of accessing this table from a Java class, by writing methods to store to, and fetch from, the table.

## 10.1.2 Java code to store and fetch "array of strings"

We shall define a class to represent the countries, and the class will include methods to instantiate a country from the database and to store a new country in the database. The skeleton of the class definition is shown below:

```java
package mypackage1;

import java.sql.*;

public class MyCountry  {

    private String name;
    private int popn;
    private String[] cities;

    private static Connection connection;

    public MyCountry(String n, int p, String[] c) {
      name = n;
      popn = p;
      cities = c;
    }

    public void connect() {
        // method to establish a database connection, to be held in the
                // static variable
    }

    public void disconnect() {
        // method to close the database connection and update the
                // static variable
    }

    public boolean store () throws SQLException {
        // method to insert this country into the database
    }
```

```
public static MyCountry fetch(String countryName) throws
    SQLException {
    // method to fetch from the database the country with the given name,
    // and instantiate a new instance of this class
}

public String toString() {
    // return the representation of the object as a string
}

}
```

The scope of the class is limited, but it will allow us to create new instances in Java and store them in the database; and to retrieve existing instances from the database into Java. The toString() method will enable us to display the retrieved countries in a convenient format.

Let us now consider how we can develop the code for the two key methods of the class, namely fetch() and store(). Notice that we have defined store() to be an instance method, because it is necessary to first create an instance in Java before we can store it in the database. On the other hand, we define fetch() as a class method because in that case the instance does not initially exist in Java (it will be created by the method). Notice also that we have imported only the package java.sql, giving us access to the standard JDBC interface. In this way, whenever we use any of the Oracle extensions of the interface, we shall have to explicitly state the full name of the class. It should be very clear, therefore, when we are diverging from the JDBC standard. Both methods declare that they may throw a SQLException. We are therefore assigning responsibility to the client class for handling any exceptions which may be thrown during processing.

The fetch() method follows a similar pattern to that which we would use when retrieving from columns of simple type. We iterate over the result set, and fetch each column in turn. Whereas getString() and getInt() are used to obtain the values of the name and population columns respectively, we use getObject() to obtain the value of the cities column. We cast the result of getObject() to java.sql.Array, the interface representing the SQL type ARRAY. The usual implementation of this type is as a logical pointer to the array data, which means that a further operation is needed to fetch the data themselves. JDBC defines a method getArray() to obtain a Java array from

211

an instance of java.sql.Array. Since the array contains only strings, we can cast that array to the type String[]. The implementation of the method is shown below:

```
public static MyCountry fetch(String countryName) throws SQLException
{
    PreparedStatement  pstmt = connection.prepareStatement(
        "SELECT name, population, cities FROM country " +
        "WHERE name = ? " );
    pstmt.setString( 1, countryName ); // Bind the country name
    // Execute Query
    ResultSet rset = pstmt.executeQuery();
    java.sql.Array cities;
    MyCountry tc = null;
    // Retrieve the CITY_LIST collection from the ResultSet.
    if ( rset.next( ) ) {
        String nm = rset.getString(1);
        int pop = rset.getInt(2);
        cities = (java.sql.Array) rset.getObject( 3 );
        String[] clist = (String[]) cities.getArray( );
        tc = new MyCountry(nm,pop,clist);
    }
    rset.close();
    pstmt.close();
    return tc;
}
```

Note that a pre-condition of the method is that a connection has been established before it is called. We are assigning to the client class responsibility for ensuring that connection is not null. There is also a danger of returning a null result from the method, if it is passed a country name which does not exist in the database. The client class will therefore have to check for a non-null result, to avoid the risk of a null-pointer exception.

The store() method requires knowledge of the data type cityList which was defined in Oracle. This is done through the class oracle.sql.ArrayDescriptor, which is responsible for making SQL array types known to the Java program. The method createDescriptor() is a factory method which tells Java to look up the name in the database, and

212

determine the characteristics of the array. Having created a descriptor, we can build an instance of oracle.sql.ARRAY from the Java array. The class oracle.sql.ARRAY is Oracle's implementation of the java.sql.Array interface. Once we have an instance of oracle.sql.ARRAY, we can use the setArray() method to bind the array in the prepared statement which will insert the data. The implementation of store() is given below:

```
public boolean store () throws SQLException {

    oracle.sql.ArrayDescriptor descriptor =
    oracle.sql.ArrayDescriptor.createDescriptor
        ("CITYLIST", connection);
    oracle.sql.ARRAY cityArray = new oracle.sql.ARRAY (descriptor,
        connection, cities);
    PreparedStatement ps = connection.prepareStatement(
        "insert into country (name, population, cities) values (?,?,?)");
    ps.setString(1,name);
    ps.setInt(2,popn);
    ps.setArray(3,cityArray);
    boolean res = ps.execute();
    connection.commit();
    return res;
}
```

The method returns a boolean result, to indicate whether or not the data were inserted into the table successfully. It is likely that an exception would be thrown in the event of the insertion failing, but it is still good practice to return a result explicitly to the client class.

The methods store() and fetch() have illustrated how an array can be passed from Java to Oracle, or from Oracle to Java. The same approaches can be used to implement other operations which might be needed, such as updating the array. To update the population and list of cities for a particular country, we could call an UPDATE statement as follows:

```
public int update () throws SQLException {
    oracle.sql.ArrayDescriptor descriptor =
    oracle.sql.ArrayDescriptor.createDescriptor
        ("CITYLIST", connection);
    oracle.sql.ARRAY cityArray = new oracle.sql.ARRAY (descriptor,
```

```
        connection, cities);
    PreparedStatement ps = connection.prepareStatement(
            "update country set population = ?, cities = ? where name = ?");
    ps.setString(3,name);
    ps.setInt(1,popn);
    ps.setArray(2,cityArray);
    int res = ps.executeUpdate();
    connection.commit();
    return res;
}
```

In this case, the update() method is returning the number of rows updated
by the execution of the database update. As long as we define name to be
the primary key of the table, this result should be either 0 or 1, depending
on whether the specified country exists in the database.

### 10.1.3 Oracle code for collection of structured objects

The example described above did not require much more coding than that
which we used for accessing a table with simple data types. We needed to
create an array descriptor in order to pass the array to Oracle, and we
needed a two-step process (getObject() followed by getArray()) to fetch the
array back into the Java space, but otherwise the code was all quite familiar.
Indeed, we do not require any additional constructs to handle arrays whose
elements are strings or numbers. Things get a bit more interesting, though,
when we are dealing with an array of user-defined objects. Let us consider
a similar example in which each country still maintains a list of cities, but
this time the cities are to be objects which have a population as well as a
name. On the Oracle side, we first need to define a data type for the cities:

    create type city as object (name varchar2(20), population integer);

We then need to define the collection type. This time we'll use a nested
table, though a VARRAY could also have been used.

    create type cityList2 as table of city;

214

To complete the definition on the Oracle side, we define the table country2. Since cities is defined as a nested table, we need to include a storage clause for it.

```
create table country2 (name varchar2(20), population integer, cities
    cityList2)
nested table cities store as city2;
```

**10.1.4 Java code for reading from and storing to collection of objects**

<u>(a) the class for Country information</u>

On the Java side, we shall once again define a class to represent the countries, and the class will include methods to instantiate a country from the database and to store a new country in the database. The skeleton of the class definition is shown below:

```
package mypackage1;

import java.sql.*;

public class MyCountry2 {

    private String name;
    private int popn;
    private City[] cities;

    private static Connection connection;

    public MyCountry2(String n, int p, City[] c) {
      name = n;
      popn = p;
      cities = c;
    }

    public void connect() {
        // method to establish a database connection, to be held in the
        // static variable
    }
```

```
    public void disconnect() {
        // method to close the database connection and update the
        // static variable
    }

    public boolean store () throws SQLException {
        // method to insert this country into the database
    }

    public static MyCountry2 fetch(String countryName) throws
        SQLException {
        // method to fetch from the database the country with the given name,
        // and instantiate a new instance of this class
    }

    public String toString() {
        // return the representation of the object as a string
    }

}
```

Again, the key methods are store() and fetch(), so we shall look at the implementation of those two methods in some detail. It turns out that store() can be implemented in just the same way as before. The fact that we are dealing with a collection of objects, rather than a collection of strings, makes no difference to the code: in either case, we create an array descriptor to retrieve the type definition from the database.

```
public boolean store () throws SQLException {
    oracle.sql.ArrayDescriptor descriptor =
        oracle.sql.ArrayDescriptor.createDescriptor ("CITYLIST2",
        connection);
    oracle.sql.ARRAY cityArray = new oracle.sql.ARRAY (descriptor,
        connection, (Object[])cities);
    PreparedStatement ps = connection.prepareStatement
        ("insert into country2 values (?,?,?)");
    ps.setString(1,name);
    ps.setInt(2,popn);
    ps.setArray(3,cityArray);
```

```
    boolean res = ps.execute();
    connection.commit();
    return res;
}
```

This time it is the fetch() method which requires us to use some additional classes and constructs. Recall that, when retrieving a collection of strings, we invoked getObject() to get a logical pointer to the array, followed by getArray() to populate the array with the strings. Unfortunately, that approach does not suffice when dealing with a collection of objects. Instead, we need to iterate over the elements of the SQL array, and extract the individual fields of each array element. To iterate over the array elements, we make use of the getResultSet() method of the java.sql.Array interface. Then, invoking getObject() on the current element of the result set, we retrieve the array element as a Struct. A Struct contains one value for each attribute of the SQL type which it represents. To make sense of it, we need to know the structure of the particular type which we are retrieving. In this case we know that it is a City, with the first attribute being a string (name) and the second attribute being a number (population). We use the getAttributes() method to obtain the attributes of a Struct as an array. We then cast each attribute to the appropriate type, and create an instance of the Java class City. Since we don't know in advance how many cities are going to be in the collection, we are collecting the cities in an ArrayList. When all of the cities have been retrieved, we convert the ArrayList to a Java array and construct the instance of MyCountry2. The complete implementation of fetch() is shown below:

```
public static MyCountry2 fetch(String countryName) throws
    SQLException{
    // Prepare a query to fetch cities for a selected country
    PreparedStatement pstmt = connection.prepareStatement(
        "SELECT name, population, cities FROM COUNTRY2 " +
        "WHERE name = ? " );
    pstmt.setString( 1, countryName ); // Bind the country name
    // prepare a query with the selected values.
    MyCountry2 tc = null;
    ResultSet rset = pstmt.executeQuery( ); // execute the query.
    Array cities;
    // Retrieve the CITY_LIST collection from the ResultSet.
    if ( rset.next( ) ) {
```

```
        String nm = rset.getString(1);
        int pp = rset.getInt(2);
        cities = (Array) rset.getObject( 3 );
        // define collection for holding cities
        java.util.ArrayList ccoll = new java.util.ArrayList();
        ResultSet res1 = cities.getResultSet();
        // Loop and retrieve all cities.
        int i = 0;
        while (res1.next()) {
            Struct objstruct = (Struct)res1.getObject(2);
            // get the attributes in the Struct objstruct.
            Object[] objval = objstruct.getAttributes( );
            // Retrieve individual attributes.
            String cityName = (String) objval[ 0 ];
            int pop = ((Number) objval[ 1 ]).intValue();
            ccoll.add ( new City (cityName, pop));
        }
         res1.close();
        City[] clist = (City[])ccoll.toArray (new City[0]);
        tc = new MyCountry2 (nm, pp, clist);
    }
    // close the statement
    pstmt.close();
    return tc;
}
```

When we fetch an instance of a user-defined type into a Struct, it is necessary to have a class on the Java side which implements the java.sql.SQLData interface. This interface specifies the following methods:

- getSQLTypeName() gives the name of the SQL type corresponding to this class
- readSQL() specifies how to read from the SQL type into the Java class
- writeSQL() specifies how to write from the Java class to the SQL type

For this example, we define a class City as follows:

(b) the class for City information

```
package mypackage1;

import java.sql.*;

public class City implements SQLData {

    String name;
    int popn;

    public City(String n, int p) {
        name = n;
        popn = p;
    }

    public String getSQLTypeName() throws SQLException
    {
     return "CITY";
    }

    public void readSQL (SQLInput stream, String typeName)
          throws SQLException
    {
     name = stream.readString();
     popn = stream.readInt();
    }

    public void writeSQL(SQLOutput stream) throws SQLException
    {
     stream.writeString(name);
     stream.writeInt(popn);
    }
}
```

We have presented solutions to the problem of fetching arrays from a database into Java, using the standard JDBC interface. These solutions can be implemented on any JDBC-compliant DBMS, though some systems have defined their own extensions to JDBC which provide alternative implementations. Though there can be performance advantages in using the

DBMS-specific extensions, the standard interface has the advantage of DBMS independence; it also offers fairly straightforward implementations.

## 10.2 Accessing large objects

In this section, we shall present an approach to passing large objects between Java and the database. JDBC defines the interfaces java.sql.Clob (to represent the SQL type CLOB) and java.sql.Blob (to represent the SQL type BLOB). We shall present separate solutions for reading and writing each of these types. As with collection types, the DBMS vendors provide their own implementations for these interfaces and their own extensions to the JDBC standard. Again, our approach is one which is defined for an Oracle database, but we shall keep to the JDBC standard as far as possible. Consequently, only small modifications should be needed in order to make these solutions work with a different DBMS.

### 10.2.1 Oracle for large objects

Suppose we have a number of maps of different areas, which we want to store in a database table. We also have a number of documents, in plain text format, which we want to store in another database table. The maps, whether they be in JPEG, TIFF, GIF, BMP or some other format, can be held in the database in a column of type BLOB; the documents will be held in a column of type CLOB. As the basis for our solution, we shall define the following tables and sequences:

Create table mymap (key integer, map blob);

Create table mydoc (key integer, doc clob);

Create sequence blob_seq;

Create sequence clob_seq;

The table MYMAP will be used for storing BLOB values, and has an integer key for the selecting the row of interest. The key has no semantic meaning, and values will be assigned from the sequence BLOB_SEQ. The Blob values will be the content of image files, each holding a map of a different area. The table MYDOC will be used for storing CLOB values, and also has an integer key for selecting the row of interest. This time the key values will be assigned from the sequence CLOB_SEQ. The Clob values will be the content of text files, each holding a different document.

### 10.2.2 Outline of Java class for large objects

The skeleton class definition is as follows:

```
package mypackage1;

import java.sql.*;
import java.io.*;

public class LobAccess  {

    private static Connection connection;

    public LobAccess() {
    }

public int writeBlob (InputStream inStream) throws SQLException,
IOException {
    // read binary data from the given input stream
    // (typically reading from a file)
    // and write to the MYMAP table
}

 public int writeClob (Reader reader) throws SQLException, IOException {
    // read character data from the given reader,
    // and write to the MYDOC table
}

public String fetchClob (int keyVal) throws SQLException,  IOException {
    // return the document stored in the row of MYDOC
    // whose key is keyVal
}

public void fetchBlob (int keyVal) throws SQLException, IOException {
    // fetch the map stored in the row of MYMAP whose key is keyVal
    // and store in the file mymap<keyVal>.gif
```

```
        }
}
```

As with the collection examples, we are holding the database connection as a static variable of the class. We are again importing the package java.sql, which means that the code can use the standard JDBC interface – but any use of the Oracle extensions will need to be made explicit by use of the fully qualified class name.

When storing large objects, we shall usually want to take the content of a file and store it in the database. To make the methods more general, though, we are specifying the input as a stream: an input stream in the case of Blobs, and a reader in the case of Clobs. We shall also use an output stream for writing to the database, so that we do not have to pass the entire object as a single chunk. When retrieving large objects from the database, we need to specify the key value corresponding to the object to be fetched. When fetching a Clob, the object will be fetched into a Java string (it is possible to create very long strings in Java, as long as sufficient memory is available, so it is reasonable to hold the result as a string unless the Clobs are expected to be extremely large). When fetching a Blob, the object will be saved to a file. This will allow us to write to an output stream, without ever materialising the complete object within Java.

### 10.2.3 Writing large character objects

When writing Clobs to the database from Java, we need to use some Oracle-specific features. The first thing we require is a way to create a new Clob in the database. Oracle provides the construct EMPTY_CLOB() to create a new Clob with no content. Once we have created an empty Clob, we shall open an output stream on it in order to write the required content to the database.

To insert a new row into the MYDOC table, we are going to have to create a new key as well as a new Clob. Creating the key is straightforward (we get the next value from the appropriate sequence) but we need to also know the value of the key so that we can write to the correct row later. A simple INSERT statement would not accomplish that, so we instead create a callable statement which will return the assigned key value through an OUT parameter. This could be done by creating a stored procedure, but we have instead built a simple PL/SQL string and passed that string to the database in the callable statement. Having got the key value from the result of the callable statement, we use it to build a query which will retrieve the row that has just been inserted. We add "FOR UPDATE" at the end of the query in order to lock the row while we write to the Clob column. From the result set of the query, we then use the getClob() method to get hold of the clob column as an instance of java.sql.Clob, which is usually implemented as a logical pointer to the Clob. Next we obtain an output stream on the Clob data, so that we can write to the database column. Since the document may be quite large, we use a character buffer to transfer the document in small chunks. We use the reader which was given as parameter to writeClob() to obtain chunks of data, which can be written in turn to the Clob. The complete implementation of writeClob() is shown below:

```
public int writeClob (Reader reader) throws SQLException, IOException
{
    CallableStatement insert = connection.prepareCall(
      `"DECLARE retKey number; "+
       "BEGIN INSERT INTO mydoc (key, doc) "+
       "VALUES(clob_seq.nextVal, EMPTY_CLOB())"+
      "RETURNING key INTO retKey; ?:=retKey; END;");

    insert.registerOutParameter (1, Types.INTEGER);
    insert.execute();
    int keyVal = insert.getInt(1);

    // Retrieve the row just inserted, and lock it for insertion of the CLOB
    Statement select = connection.createStatement();
    ResultSet lob = select.executeQuery(
        "SELECT doc FROM mydoc WHERE key = " + keyVal +
       " FOR UPDATE");

    if ( lob.next() ) {
      Clob newClob = lob.getClob(1);
      Writer clobWriter =
        ((oracle.sql.CLOB)newClob).getCharacterOutputStream();
      // Buffer to hold chunks of data to being written to the Clob.
      char[] buffer = new char[10* 1024];

      // Read a chunk of data from the input stream,
```

223

```
   // and write the chunk to the Clob column output stream.
   // Repeat until file has been fully read.
     int nread = 0; // Number of bytes read
     while( (nread= reader.read(buffer)) != -1 ) // Read from input stream
       clobWriter.write(buffer, 0, nread); // Write to Clob

     clobWriter.close();
   }
   select.close();
   insert.close();
   connection.commit();
   return keyVal;
}
```

### 10.2.4 Writing large binary objects

The writeBlob() method follows the same approach as writeClob(). The
main difference in the case of a Blob is that we need to write bytes rather
than characters. We therefore create a binary output stream for writing the
Blob, and use an array of bytes as the buffer. The code is shown below:

```
public int writeBlob (InputStream inStream) throws SQLException,
IOException
{
   CallableStatement insert = connection.prepareCall(
       "DECLARE retKey number; "+
       "BEGIN INSERT INTO mymap (key, map) "+
       "VALUES(blob_seq.nextVal, EMPTY_BLOB())"+
       "RETURNING key INTO retKey; ?:=retKey; END;");

   insert.registerOutParameter (1, Types.INTEGER);
   insert.execute(); // Execute SQL statement
   int keyVal = insert.getInt(1);

   // Retrieve the row just inserted, and lock it for insertion of the BLOB
   Statement stmt = connection.createStatement();
   ResultSet lob = stmt.executeQuery(
       "SELECT map FROM mymap WHERE key = " + keyVal +
         " FOR UPDATE");
```

```
if( lob.next() ) {
    Blob newBlob = lob.getBlob(1);
    OutputStream blobOutputStream =
        ((oracle.sql.BLOB)newBlob).getBinaryOutputStream();

    // Buffer to hold chunks of data to be written to the Blob.
    byte[] buffer = new byte[10* 1024];

    // Read a chunk of data from the sample file input stream,
    // and write the chunk to the Blob column output stream
    // Repeat until file has been fully read.
    int nread = 0; // Number of bytes read
    while( (nread= inStream.read(buffer)) != -1 )
        // Read from input stream
        blobOutputStream.write(buffer, 0, nread); // Write to Blob

    blobOutputStream.close();
}
stmt.close();
insert.close();
connection.commit();
return keyVal;
}
```

### 10.2.5 Fetching large character objects

Whereas our methods for storing large objects made use of some Oracle-specific extensions to JDBC, we are going to restrict ourselves to standard JDBC in implementing the methods for retrieving large objects into Java. Fetching a large character object is, in a sense, just a particular case of fetching a string. But when a column is of CLOB type, it is stored in a different way from a VARCHAR column and therefore needs to be accessed slightly differently. In addition, the volume of data to be fetched is typically much larger, which also calls for a different approach.

Suppose we query a table to retrieve the value of a clob-valued column from the row with a given key value. From the result set, we use getClob() instead of getString() to access the clob-valued column. Whereas

225

getString() retrieves a string from a VARCHAR column, getClob() retrieves a java.sql.Clob. From the Clob, we use getCharacterStream() to create a reader, which can be used to obtain the actual data. Since the Clob may be quite large, we shall transfer it from the database in chunks of 1024 bytes. These chunks are concatenated using a string buffer, in order to build the full result. The code for fetchClob() is shown below.

```
public String fetchClob (int keyVal) throws SQLException,  IOException
{
   Statement stmt = null;
   String clobData = null;
   // Now build up the SQL query from the inputs provided
   stmt = connection.createStatement();
   // execute the query to get a handle on the CLOB
   ResultSet rs = stmt.executeQuery (
       "SELECT doc FROM mydoc WHERE key = "+keyVal);
   if (rs.next())
   {
      Clob clob = rs.getClob(1);
      // read 1024 chars at a time
      Reader clobStream = clob.getCharacterStream();
      int charsRead = 0;
      StringBuffer clobBuf = new StringBuffer();
      char[] buf = new char[1024];
      while ((charsRead = clobStream.read(buf)) != -1)
         clobBuf.append (buf, 0, charsRead);
      clobData = clobBuf.toString();
      clobStream.close();
   }
   rs.close();
   stmt.close();
   return clobData;
}
```

## 10.2.6 Fetching large binary objects

The technique for reading a Blob column is quite similar to that for reading a Clob. After obtaining the result set, the getBlob() method is used to get the Blob object which again is usually implemented by a logical pointer to the Blob data. We then open an input stream on the blob data, and an output stream on the file to which the Blob is to be saved. This allows us to read chunks of the Blob into a buffer, and write each chunk to the file, without ever having to build the entire object in the Java environment. This approach is memory-efficient, and scales easily to very large Blob files. The code for the fetchBlob() method is shown below:

```java
public void fetchBlob (int keyVal) throws SQLException, IOException
{
    Statement stmt = connection.createStatement();
    // Query mymap for the selected map
    ResultSet lobDetails = stmt.executeQuery(
        "SELECT map FROM mymap WHERE key = "+keyVal);
    // Check if LOB columns exist
    if( lobDetails.next() ) {
        // LOB details exist
        // fetch map
        Blob blob = lobDetails.getBlob(1);
        // Open a stream to read the Blob data
        InputStream blobStream = blob.getBinaryStream();
        // get user home folder name
        String userHome = System.getProperty("user.home");
        System.out.println ("Directory for BLOB files is: "+userHome);
        // append the file name with user home directory, file separator and
        // file extension GIF
        String fileName =
            userHome+File.separator+"mymap"+keyVal+".gif";
        // Open a file stream to save the Blob data
        FileOutputStream fileOutStream = new FileOutputStream(fileName);
        // Read from the Blob data input stream, and write to the file output
        // stream
        byte[] buffer = new byte[1024];
            // buffer holding bytes to be transferred
        int nbytes = 0; // Number of bytes read
        while( (nbytes = blobStream.read(buffer)) != -1 )
            // Read from Blob stream
            fileOutStream.write(buffer, 0, nbytes); // Write to file stream
        // Flush and close the streams
        fileOutStream.flush();
        fileOutStream.close();
```

```
        blobStream.close();
    }
}
```

Whereas the fetchClob() method retrieved a document into a Java string, fetchBlob() copies an image from the database into the local file system. This approach assumes that the application can easily process an image that is stored in a file. The assumption is reasonable because Sun provides a suite of optional packages which can be used to implement complex imaging requirements based on images stored in files. Java Advanced Imaging (JAI) provides a set of object-oriented interfaces that supports a simple, high-level programming model which allows images to be manipulated easily in Java applications and applets. JAI goes beyond the functionality of traditional imaging APIs to provide a high-performance, platform-independent, extensible image processing framework. The Java Image I/O API provides a pluggable architecture for working with images stored in files and accessed across the network. Both JAI and the Java Image I/O API provide straightforward interfaces for reading an image from a file. In the case of JAI, an image can be read from a file as follows into an instance of the class java.awt.RenderedImage:

```
RenderedImage image = (RenderedImage)JAI.create("fileload", fileName);
```

Having obtained the rendered image, it is quite straightorward to display the image using the AWT. JAI provides a variety of additional features for supporting more sophisticated image processing requirements.

# INDEX OF CONCEPTS

www.ingramcontent.com/pod-product-compliance
Lightning Source LLC
Chambersburg PA
CBHW051231050326
40689CB00007B/885